FRED learns about
COMPUTERS

𝔗𝔥𝔢 𝔆𝔥𝔯𝔬𝔫𝔦𝔠𝔩𝔢𝔯
Lord High Keeper of the Royal Fredlandic Archives

MACDONALD & EVANS

Macdonald & Evans Ltd
Estover, Plymouth PL6 7PZ

First published 1978
Second edition 1981
Reprinted 1982

© Macdonald & Evans Ltd 1981

0 7121 0636 7

HAVE YOU READ:

FRED learns Book-keeping
FRED learns The New Mathematics
FRED learns Modern Economics
FRED learns Basic Statistics
FRED learns Accounts

Printed in Great Britain by
Hollen Street Press Ltd.,
Slough

PREFACE

"A little knowledge is a dangerous thing, but ignorance is lethal."   — *Old Fredlandic Proverb*

Fredbooks are just the books to be read by people with no time to read.

Well not exactly no time at all — rather no time to spare for laboriously climbing the mountains of words that seem inseparable from a reasonable understanding of most technical subjects. For these people there are Fredbooks. Fredbooks aim to convey quickly and as painlessly as possible the broad outline of the subject. By displaying pictorial analogies within the text, by developing a topic in the form it would naturally evolve in ordinary day-to-day conversation, and by concentrating first, foremost and at all times on what the reader *wants* to know rather than what the writer feels he ought to know, it is hoped that this aim is successful.

One thing perhaps should be made clear from the outset. Fredbooks, though simple in style, are substantial in content. If a job's worth doing it's worth doing well — even if that job is to give no more than a general but comprehensive survey of a topic. Inevitably there will be some simplification since the effective stripping of a subject to its essential core cannot simultaneously retain all the confusing proliferations that exist in real life. But this simplification, we believe, leads to deeper, not shallower, understanding. And for those people who insist that it is not possible to have profundity with fun nor comprehension of the complex without dreariness there's plenty of alternative literature available. Fredbooks are for the others.

Finally we must acknowledge our deep gratitude to the Chronicler, Royal Archivist to the Kingdom of Fredland. But for the Chronicler's dedication to the task of observing Fred's educational progress under the guidance of Rufus, in the various subjects that interest him, and his subsequent release to us of the records of his observations, there would and could have been no Fredbooks.

And that, we suspect, would have been a pity.

The Publishers

FREDLAND: FACTS & FACES

For the benefit of the non-Fredlandic reader we introduce below some of the more important features of Fredland.

FRED

Rufus, Professor of Allthings, University of Fredland. Fred's guide and philosopher.

The Fredstick (F or f) — the unit of currency in Fredland. It is subdivided into 100 Chips.

Fredlanders. The hoi-polloi of Fredland. Immediately recognisable by their geometric shapes.

Polybits (℔) — The unique national product. Used in every circumstance where round commodities (such as cheeses, wheels and self-winding, all-weather, non-slip sun-dials) are called for.

Multiparts (℔) — Like the Polybit, this can be used in a multitude of circumstances, but needing a *square* product (such as bread slices, office windows and supersonic aircraft tail-planes).

CONTENTS

1. WHAT'S IT ALL ABOUT, THEN?

"Computers," snorted Fred contemptuously. "Bah! let me tell you — a computer is as stupid as a donkey!"

"I'd say that was a gross slander on the whole of the asinine species," remarked Rufus mildly.

Fred looked nonplussed.

"You agree they're stupid, then?" he pressed.

"Certainly I do. In fact," reflected Rufus, "I suppose the ultimate in intellectual denigration is to assert that someone is as stupid as a computer."

The legend of the F0.00 bill

"It's not often you and I see eye to eye on modern developments," said Fred. "Well, now, I've a story to confirm our views that'll make your hair stand on end. Last quarter Freda was away from home for the whole time. As a result she used no electricity and, as she has no standing charge, her debt to the Fredland Electricity Corporation was nothing. Now, do you know what? They sent her a bill — for all of F0.00!!"

"It was what she owed them," Rufus pointed out.

7

"Ah, but that wasn't the end of it. Three weeks later she got a final demand for F0.00 and a letter threatening to take her to court for non-payment."

"A logical step," observed Rufus.

"So she went in to ask them what was going on. Then they told her that unless there was a receipt for the invoiced amount bearing a cheque payment reference number the computer would regard her as a defaulting customer."

"So she took out her cheque book," said Rufus, " wrote out a cheque for F0.00, gave it to the cashier in exchange for her receipt, and heard nothing further."

"How do you know," exclaimed an astonished Fred.

"It's an old computer legend," yawned Rufus. "Heard it dozens of times."

"Well, perhaps you have, but doesn't it just go to show how stupid a computer is?"

"Yes and no. If a computer is instructed to treat as a defaulter a customer who fails to give a cheque in payment of the correct amount owing it will do just that — regardless of the senselessness of the action in this specific case. But, Fred — is it the computer that's stupid or the person who gave it the original instructions? The fact is that computers only do what they're told — neither more nor less. But look here, I'm sure you've not come over merely to lay bare the intellectual inadequacies of the computer world."

The true reason for Fred's visit

"No — that would take all day," remarked Fred cheerfully. "You're quite right, though — I'm really here because my boss said I ought to know a bit about computers."

"Which bit?" asked Rufus caustically.

Fred blinked.

"Just a bit," he answered at last. "A bit. A little. Surely you know what he means."

"I must confess, I suspect the worst. Tell me, *why* did he send you?"

"Don't really know," admitted Fred. "My guess, though, is that he's going to buy a computer one day and feels he'd like his managers to have some advance ideas about what it will do."

"If he buys a computer in his present state of ignorance," said Rufus coldly, "he'll become both a sadder and wiser man, that's for sure. Well now, Fred, I take it that he doesn't expect you to build one yourself?"

"Lord, no. You know what a duffer I am about anything electrical."

"And you're an equal duffer at mathematics and science so it's not likely that he'll be looking to you to use a computer in those two fields."

"No," agreed Fred. "I'm a business manager."

"So what *you* need to know is how to use a computer in a business situation."

"That's about it. And I remember now — one thing my boss did say at the time was, 'Fred, find out what a computer can do'."

All the things a computer can do

To Fred's surprise this last remark of his was followed by a very long silence. At last Rufus replied.

"That's an extremely difficult thing to do," he said slowly. "What you have to realise is that a computer is more of a tool than a machine. Tell me, Fred, what can a pen do?"

"Well, write, of course."

"So a computer can compute."

"That's no answer," Fred complained.

"It's as good as yours was," replied Rufus spiritedly. "You see, just as a pen can write sublime poetry so a computer can approach unbelievable sophistication in the preparation of business information. Both, of course, can produce rubbish and the scope of each is wholly determined by the human controlling it. I should perhaps emphasise that, like a pen, a computer has to be guided every bit of the way. It has absolutely no ability at all to make a decision for itself. And I need hardly add that neither has the ability to open a bottle of beer."

Fred still looked rather lost so in an effort to help him further Rufus went on to explain that a computer can do a great many things provided that:

* *everything* it does relates to the *manipulation of data* and nothing else. In other words, it can only handle numbers, letters and symbols.

* *everything* it is required to do can be, and is, *precisely specified in terms of instructions.* If you yourself can't tell the computer exactly what to do at every step in its operation, it can't do it.

* *everything* it handles is in an *objective quantifiable form.* A computer cannot tell you which is the most beautiful girl in the room — though if you tell the computer that the most beautiful girl is the one whose statistics most closely approach 36-26-36 it may well be able to reach a decision.

"So you see," concluded Rufus, "in the business field a computer can make computations and provide information in sales accounting, credit control, stock control, production control, seat reservations and payrolls, while slightly outside that field it can be used for vehicular and traffic control, weather forecasting, school-timetable compilation. . . . "

"All right, all right," cried Fred. "It seems that anything a human can do with paper and pencil a computer can do."

"Generally speaking, yes, but not in every case. It can't, for instance, draw creative pictures — though it can be made to draw *original* pictures by producing lines based on chance numbers."

"A sort of random art, eh?"

"I prefer to restrict the word 'art' to more aesthetically teleological entities," sniffed Rufus.

"Which brings us to my next worry," said Fred. "The jargon."

Computer English

"Ah, yes, the jargon," repeated Rufus. "I will admit there's a great deal of it used between computer personnel. Well, Fred,

I promise you that I'll try and keep this to a minimum. But now, I think, might be an appropriate moment to look at a few common words — one or two because I'll need to use them in our future discussions and the rest because you're likely to meet them being used by other people anyway.''

"I suspect," said Fred, "it's going to be the case of new words for old in a number of instances.''

"You're perfectly right. Indeed, our first word, the verb *'to access'* falls in this very category since it means no more than 'get at'. So when we talk about one piece of data being accessed as quickly as another we mean it is 'got at' as quickly. Inevitably such a general word creeps into a number of other terms — such as *access time,* which means the time it takes to get at the thing accessed, and *sequential access* and *random access* where the former means that the item accessed is got at by running through a sequence in order and the latter that you can access the item you want at random.''

"I never do things at random," said Fred.

"No, I don't mean like that. I mean you can have access to your data at once in any order without having to run through

any sequence — such as accessing 5 by going via 1, 2, 3 and 4. Next, do you know what is meant by 'dedication'?''

"Of course. As a matter of fact I was once told that a computer unit had been dedicated to me. Rather sweet, I thought.''

"No, no. Computer *dedication* means 'reserved exclusively for'. If I remember rightly, the unit to which you refer belonged to the company who used to employ you as an ice-cream salesman — and it was dedicated to you because it had to operate full time sorting out your takings muddles."

"Yes, I remember now that I did have trouble. They were always muttering something about 'validation', whatever that meant."

"*Validation,* Fred, means checking to see if the data given to the computer is correct or not. For instance if you dated a form 31st September a validation check (which the computer itself makes) would result in your form being rejected since there are only thirty days in September."

"Come to think of it, they did used to object to me working an eight-day week. What they forgot was that Sunday was double-time."

"Yes, validation would involve rejecting an eight-day week," remarked Rufus drily.

"But I don't see how it can check that a sales figure of 101 should be 102 or not. I mean, if the computer knows that right from the start there's no point in me telling it."

"It certainly can't do that. But it can check to see if your data is reasonable. So if 100 was about your usual day's sales then sales of, say, 1000 would be queried."

"On the grounds that I may have written a nought too many. Yes, that did happen on occasions."

Rufus made no further comment but merely went on to explain that *format* meant no more than the arrangement of data — either as regards the layout of a printed document or the layout of the data within the computer.

Hardware and software

"But of greatest importance at this stage," continued Rufus, "is for you to distinguish between 'hardware' and 'software'."

" 'Hardware' is an ordinary word," observed Fred. "But software. . . . Sounds like a fur-lined boot to me."

"No, 'software' is really used in contrast to 'hardware'. And *hardware* is all the electrical and mechanical parts of the computer — the parts you can kick and drop on the floor. But the *software* is the 'non-hardware', that is, the programs and internal control systems. To take a culinary analogy, the hardware

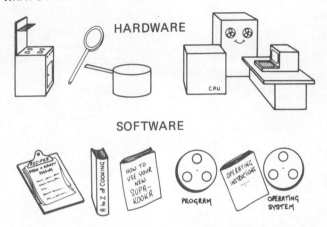

HARDWARE

SOFTWARE

would be your cooker, pots and pans, bowls, spoons and knives while your software would be your recipes, cooking techniques and instructions for working your cooker."

"I can drop a book of instructions on the floor," Fred pointed out.

"Yes, and you can kick a computer tape of programs. But just as the software recipes and cooker instructions *have* to be written on some sort of recording material so the software programs have to be 'written' on a corresponding piece of material. However, just as a recipe is not a piece of paper so a program is not a computer tape."

"It sounds as if software is a sort of 'all-in-the-mind' thing."

"Yes, it is certainly more akin to structured thought than to inanimate matter," conceded Rufus.

"Which is just what I said," thought Fred to himself though aloud he pointed out that cooking wasn't just pots, pans and recipes — he had to have food to cook.

"Of course," agreed Rufus. "And just as cooking is essentially the treatment of your ingredients using your culinary hardware and software, so computing is the treatment of your data using your computer hardware and software."

"I've heard of people cooking the books. . . ." said Fred thoughtfully.

"My analogy is in no way original," confessed Rufus. "Now, before you can appreciate the software side of computing it is

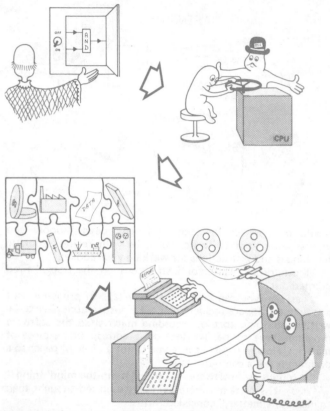

necessary for you to have some idea of how the hardware works. So I'll discuss that first — after which we'll look at the software side which involves seeing how you can give orders to your computer, and, incidentally, how it can give orders to itself. Then we'll see how the computer fits into the business 'scene', as I believe you'd call it, Fred — both in terms of organisation and also in terms of computer technique."

"Talking of cooking . . ." murmured Fred wistfully.

"But of course," said Rufus looking at his watch. "Now, Fred, they do a very pleasant Gaelic coffee in the University bar. . . ."

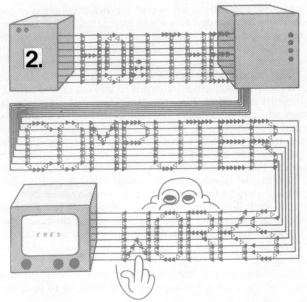

"You know," said Fred when they had returned to Rufus's office that afternoon, "in my opinion the word 'hardware' is very misleading. After all, everybody knows that really and truly there's a little man inside the computer who does it all."

"The same little man, no doubt," said Rufus sourly, "who sits in your transistor and reads you the news. No, Fred," he continued hurriedly as Fred's face began to light up with revelation, "I can assure you that it's *all* done by electronics. Now since you are not at this moment wanting to learn about electronics I don't intend to go too deeply into the technical side. But you should really know what the various pieces of hardware do and how your data is handled electronically."

How a computer talks to itself

"The first thing to appreciate, Fred, is that a 'computer' is simply the name given to a *collection* of electronic units. Indeed, rather than think of the computer as a machine, it is better to think of it as a community. Just as a community is essentially a group of individual people who can collectively be regarded as a single integrated body, so a computer is a group of individual units which can be regarded as a single integrated piece of equipment. Incidentally, the term *configuration* is given to these computer communities.

"Now human beings within a community are able to communicate with each other by means of audible or visual signals or by written symbols. Alas, computers lack such great sophistication and communication between units within a computer system is limited to an electronic component's sub-moronic ability to recognise only two electrical signal patterns — 'current on' and 'current off'. So the only way, therefore, that a computer can talk to itself is in terms of the existence of, or absence of, current. All words, numbers, visual pictures or other data must ultimately be translated into this very simple code."

"I don't follow that," said Fred. "Either there's a current or there isn't. You can't 'code' anything in that situation."

"You can switch the current on and off," Rufus pointed out.

"You mean one flick of the switch for an A and twenty-six flicks for a Z?"

"Yes — except that there is a much shorter way. Imagine, Fred, that there are three wires running from me to you, each

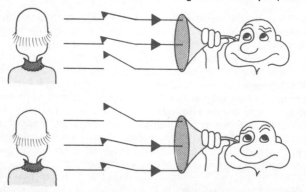

with its own switch. Now can you see that by selecting different combinations of switches I can send you different coded patterns? If I flicked just the top two switches on and off quickly the pattern you'd receive would be different from the one you'd obtain if I flicked only the bottom two switches."

"Well, yes. In fact," added Fred, trying out all the possible combinations, "there are eight different patterns — if you include the one where you don't flick any switches at all."

"Well done, Fred. Now what if we had *eight* different wires joining us?"

"Good Heavens," gasped Fred. "I can't work out how many different patterns there are there."

"One day we'll talk about combinations and then you'll be able to do it," promised Rufus. "In point of fact there are 256. So if we let one pattern stand for A, another for B. . . .''

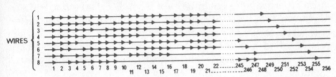

". . . We could cover all the letters from A to Z," broke in Fred excitedly, "and all the digits from 0 to 9 and still have lots of spare patterns for things like commas, full stops, asterisks, and all that. And, I suppose," Fred added as an after-thought, "computers can send an eight-wire pattern very quickly."

"They can indeed. In fact the 'flicking' is done so quickly that the resulting currents flow down the wires as a series of electrical pulses. So if, for example, we agreed that a flick of all the switches except for the second one down stood for 'F', all but the third for 'R', all but the fourth for 'E', and all but the fifth for 'D', then you can see how your name would speed down the wires."

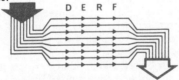

"You could almost regard the pulses as little '1's."

"Yes. In fact, in writing the code we indicate a pulse by a '1' and the absence of a pulse by a '0'. So I'd write your name as 10111111, 11011111, 11101111, 11110111."

"That looks very like the binary arithmetic we talked about once," said Fred. "You remember, where all our calculations had to be made using only digits of 0 and 1."*

*Fred learns the New Mathematics, an M & E Fredbook.

"It does. Indeed, computer operation is very much based on treating pulse patterns as binary numbers — though appreciating this is not really essential to understanding what I'm going to tell you about computers."

Bits, bytes and words

"More crucially," went on Rufus, "what needs to be appreciated is that data such as, say, the distance between two towns or the days of the week can be coded and transmitted in the form of electrical pulses. Now each pulse (or absence of a pulse where a pulse could be expected) is called a *bit*, and you have seen that a set of eight bits can be arranged in 256 different patterns. In many computer systems such a set of eight bits is called a *byte* and can be used to designate alphabetic letters, numerical digits, and a host of other useful symbols."

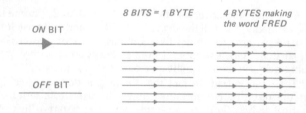

"In ordinary language," said Fred, "if we take a group of letters such as FRED we say we have a *word*. Do computers use words?"

"Oh, yes. And in exactly the same way. The only thing is that a computer 'word' can be composed of mixed characters — alphabetic letters, numeric digits, letters and digits together (which is called an *alpha-numeric* word), or even letters, digits and characters."

"Do you mean," Fred asked, "that it is possible for a 'word' to be made up simply of a collection of unusual symbols?"

"Well, of course."

"*!:+?;½/&†]]," remarked Fred.

The brain

"At the heart of every computer lies the brain," said Rufus. Having gained Fred's attention by this oddly worded introduction, Rufus explained. No matter how many different units are used in a computer's configuration, at the centre — the heart — lies what is called the Central Processing Unit (or CPU to his friends) and this unit is the brain of the whole system. In essence the CPU looks at each instruction that the computer is given and, where a calculation is to be made, selects the data designated, carries out the calculation, and sends the answer to whatever destination is instructed. Again, one should remember that the computer's real talent is speed — intellectually it is very simple. For instance, unlike humans, it cannot take four numbers and add them together in a single operation. Instead it must initially add the first and second numbers, record the answer, then add this recorded answer to the third number and so on. Dim, but fast.

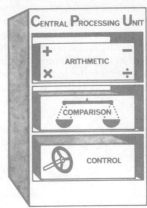

But CPUs not only calculate. Indeed, perhaps more important, they can compare two pieces of data and then take a particular course of action depending on the result of the comparison. This enables the CPU to sort out data into order or check if two pieces of information "match", e.g. if a name (of a debtor, say) taken from one source (customers' ledger) is the same as a name taken from another source (such as a sales invoice). The exploitation of this ability to take action based on such a comparison is probably one of the most valuable and distinctive qualities of the computer.

Finally the CPU controls the operations of all the parts of the computer, directing data to and from the correct places and ensuring that the whole system works in a coordinated manner.

How to feed a computer

"These pulses are all very well when you've got them," grumbled Fred. "But how do they get into the computer in the first place? I mean, how does 'Fred' get into the computer in the form of those 8-bit bytes we looked at earlier?"

"Ah," replied Rufus. "That is the job of the *input* unit. One type of unit is the 80-column card reader. This 'reads' cards having 80 columns with 12 different lines to each column. By appropriately coding the holes we can represent each of our 256 available characters by a pattern of holes punched in a column. As each card passes through the reader beams of light pass through the punched holes. These trigger off the appropriate code of pulses along the wires leading to the rest of the computer. An alternative input method involves the use of paper tape. There exactly the same principles apply, the tape usually being one inch wide and capable of being punched in eight different positions across its width. This, of course, enables bytes to be punched right across the tape directly in the 8-bit byte code — a hole giving rise to a pulse in the byte required, and the absence of a hole giving a 'no-pulse' bit."

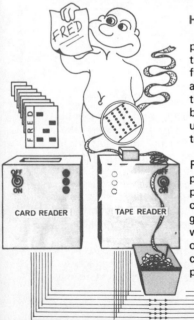

CARD READER

TAPE READER

How the computer remembers

"So we have these electrical pulses flowing along wires into the computer," said Fred thoughtfully. "But surely they can't flow around for ever. I mean, I know there's a lot of wire in the computer but the idea of all the data continually moving around is a bit difficult to swallow."

"No, of course it doesn't," replied Rufus. "But there's no theoretical problem here. Since you can use a pulse of electricity to switch on a component and subsequently regenerate the pulse by testing whether the component is switched on or not, we can arrange for the computer to 'remember' pulse patterns."

"Could you kindly be a little more explicit?"

"Well, nowadays the components I'm referring to are often tiny circuits within a silicon chip but for the sake of illustration imagine they are rings arranged in sets of eight — each set being allocated to a single 8-bit byte and each ring to a single bit in the byte. Now by leading a given byte of pulses through its set of rings so that each pulse switches on its own bit, the pattern of switched on and off rings will exactly duplicate the original pattern of the pulses, and as long as the computer itself is not switched off the pattern will remain indefinitely. And if you want to regenerate the pulse sequence you just put in an appropriate current through the eight rings and out will come the required pulses. I should, perhaps, mention that the sequences I'm referring to are those that are entered into the computer after it has been switched on at the beginning — such as the data and processing instructions for a particular job. Any information which is basic to the operation of the computer at all times is wired into it in a permanent, non-destructible form — indeed, as hardware."

"But computers are switched off from time to time, aren't they? So what happens if you want the data for another time?"

"We store it using mass storage techniques."

And Rufus went on to explain that there are two main types of storage for large amounts of data — magnetic tape and magnetic discs. The choice between these depends on the amount of data and the type and frequency of access required to that data. A *magnetic tape* unit is very similar to an ordinary tape recorder — except that the reels are held vertically. The tape comes in lengths of up to 2,400 feet. It is half an inch wide and carries a magnetisable oxide coating. When a sequence of pulses is fed into what is called the *writing head* of the unit each pulse magnetises a tiny spot on the coating immediately under the head. By designing writing heads with eight separate writing points lying at right angles across the tape and arranging for each bit of the 8-bit bytes comprising a data sequence to be wired into the appropriate writing point it is possible to write each byte in magnetic spots across the tape in sequence. To regenerate the pulses merely involves running the tape under a similar head (which is called a *reading head*) when the original sequence of pulse patterns re-emerges. And, of course, switching off the current doesn't result in taped data being lost.

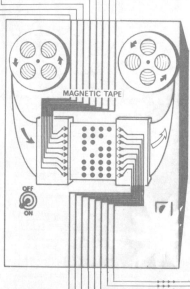

MAGNETIC TAPE

OFF
ON

"And, as you can imagine," concluded Rufus, "since a tiny area of magnetic surface is very much cheaper than even a tiny circuit in a silicon chip, mass storage is very much cheaper than the internal storage — which, by the way, we call *core* storage to distinguish it from external storage."

"Yet I suspect you'll need a lot of tape to hold any practical amount of data," remarked Fred.

"It depends. Using this method we can pack up to 6,250 bytes per inch of tape."

"My, that's a lot," exclaimed Fred. "I should think tapes are all you need for mass storage."

"Sometimes they are," replied Rufus. "But they suffer from a grave disadvantage. Access is sequential, so if you want an odd item of data (that is, if you want to have random access) then you have to run all the tape through the tape unit until you come to the data you want — and that, by computer standards, can take a very long time. However, as it happens, there is an alternative — though it is somewhat more expensive. In this other method *magnetic discs* are used. These usually come eleven at a time in a stack of what looks like long-playing records placed on top of, but separated by about an inch from, each other. Both surfaces on these discs are oxide coated and so can have magnetic information stored on them. The pack is placed on a revolving spindle, and read/write/erase heads which are located on the ends of arms attached to the unit move in and out between the discs. This enables any part of each disc to be written on or read as it revolves. A typical disc can store several million bytes of information and a computer system can have a considerable number of discs running thus allowing many millions of bytes to be accessible to the computer at any given time with only a relatively slight delay."

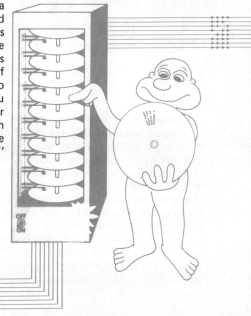

"Yet even this is a long time compared with the time it takes to access bytes in the core store," added Rufus and then went on, "Of course, if time is no object at all then you can have the computer store data in the form of cards or paper tape that punches itself."

Output — or how the computer talks to us

Fred began to smile. "As things stand now," he chuckled, "I can put data in the form of a question into the computer and the computer can work out the answer. But I don't see how it can tell me this answer. Is it going to get frustrated?"

"It won't get as frustrated in such a situation as you would," replied Rufus calmly. "But of course the computer can com-

municate with us. This is a function of the *output* units."

Output units normally take the form of a *line printer* using continuous stationery and wired into the computer system. The timing of the hammers which print out the characters is controlled by the code of bytes reaching the unit in the form of a pulse pattern. Printers can print from 120 to 160 normal characters across a line (10 characters to the inch) at speeds of up to 2,000 lines a minute and can be told to start a new page or skip a given number of lines.

Output can also be in the form of microfilm, which does not require the information to be printed first. The end result is achieved by forming the required images on a magnetic tape from which a special device can create the microfilm direct.

If a printed copy of the information is not required then it can be displayed instead on a *visual display unit* (a device like a television) linked directly to a computer.

Consoles — or how to chat with a computer

"What," asked Fred, "if I wanted to tell the computer something on the spot, as it were, without going through the business of punching up some input material?"

Fred had a good point, for when all is said and done it is still necessary to maintain human control over the computer. Only the human can recognise happenings outside the computer which will affect its operation. Perhaps all work currently running on the system needs to be stopped to allow an important job to be run immediately — or perhaps it's just time for the operator to go home.

"No problem," said Rufus. "You have a *console* which is

really no more than a typewriter (though it is sometimes a visual display unit having an incorporated keyboard) wired into the computer. By pressing a key on the console keyboard you can supply information directly to the computer so enabling outside control of the machine to be maintained. In this way you can also pass information to the computer to tell it the date and time of day, for instance. Of course, messages pass the other way, too, and the computer can tell you when a new reel of magnetic tape is required or if a card reader is jammed — things the computer can't put right on its own."

"Do we use ordinary words to talk to each other or must I learn a binary language or something?"

"Oh no. The design can be such that it talks to you in your own language," replied Rufus.

Put it together and what have you got?

"So then, a computer is an input unit, memory, mass storage unit, output unit, console and CPU all wired up together?" said Fred thoughtfully.

"In essence, yes. But we can have other units attached such as a visual display unit. And we can have a number of each kind of unit — such as half a dozen printers."

"Why, for goodness' sake?"

"Well, the computer can pour out data considerably faster than a printer can print it, so you often require more than one printer to cope with the output rate."

"Is there any part that is more crucial than another?"

"My word, yes. As I've said the CPU is the heart of the whole network — though the CPU is always reached via the memory

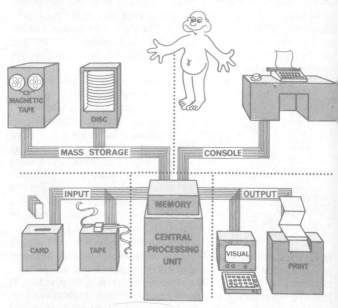

which is, of course, very closely linked to the CPU. Indeed, many people regard these two together as forming 'the computer' — so much so that all the other units are called *peripherals*."

Pulses at the gate

"I find it difficult to imagine," said Fred, shaking his head, "just how pulses floating along wires can do all these things we've been talking about."

"Ah, well, electronic wizardry and all that," replied Rufus airily. "As no doubt you appreciate, a computer can only do what it is built to do. It can, for example, multiply only if part of its circuitry is designed for multiplication. In the final analysis the computer's scope depends on its *gate circuits*, which are circuits that allow a pulse to pass out of them only if a specified pattern of pulses arrive at the gate simultaneously. It is, in fact, rather like a relay race in which the next runner can only depart if a particular group of finishing runners arrive together."

"I still don't see how that helps."

"Well, let's take the simplest case where there are just two input 'tracks'. There are three basic combinations here giving three basic types of gate. The first, called an 'OR gate', is one that gives out a pulse should a pulse arrive along *either or both* input tracks (1st OR 2nd input). The next, called an 'AND gate', is one that gives out a pulse only if pulses are received along *both* tracks (1st AND 2nd input) and the last, an intermediate one called a 'NAND gate', is one that gives out a pulse only if a pulse arrives along either track, but *not along both*.

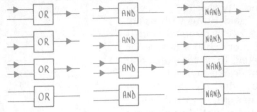

"I suppose," said Fred thoughtfully, "that by arranging a whole collection of such gates you can juggle your pulses about quite a bit."

"You can indeed. The art of circuitry design is, in fact, to use a combination of gates which will collectively perform the

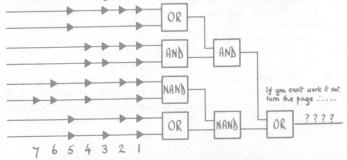

task called for. For instance, in the arithmethic unit two pulse sequences representing numbers that are to be added together will be 'gated' through the circuitry to produce a single pulse sequence representing the sum."

In passing it could perhaps be mentioned that all pulses through a computer system are synchronised by an internal clock. This "beats" very fast (in fractions of a millionth of a second) and controls all the gates so that pulses are allowed to enter and leave only when a beat is received. Thus at each clock-beat all the pulses in the computer "move on one" to the next gate.

How to talk to an absent computer

"I've got a friend," said Fred, "who knows someone whose wife works for a man whose boss sits at a typewriter all day and talks to a computer that's nowhere in sight."

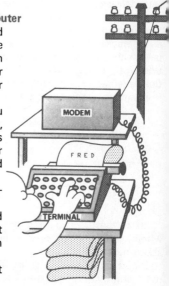

"The 'typewriter' as you call it," said Rufus with a sigh, "is actually a *terminal*, and is hardly more than a teleprinter connected to a computer and acts rather like a console."

"But the computer's nowhere in sight," insisted Fred.

"Perhaps not, but it could be in the next room, the next street, the next town, or even another country."

"My goodness, that must cost a fortune in wiring."

"On the contrary, it's very cheap. All one does is to use the existing telephone lines (and satellite communication systems if need be). The cost, then, is merely the cost of the call."

"Are you suggesting," said Fred slowly, "that you can just ring up a computer as you would a friend?"

"In effect, yes. The connection, however, must pass through a unit called a *Modem* (which stands for Modulator/Demodulator) which is necessary to convert the signals to a suitable

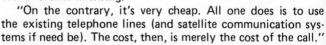

7 6 5 4 3 2 1   (so there!)

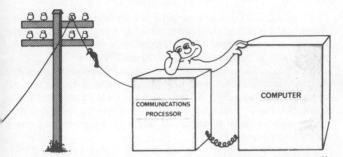

form for transmission along the telephone line and vice versa."

"A sort of 'console-in-your-own-home', eh?"

"Exactly. Operating it simply involves typing your program and data on your terminal and after the computer has done its part the answer is transmitted to the terminal again which then types out the answer without any further ado. Alternatively the answer can be given on a visual display unit."

Communications processors

"This sounds a very useful device," remarked Fred.

"It is. And indeed there is quite a rapidly growing demand for terminals. Unfortunately quite a considerable amount of processing is involved at the computer end in handling such

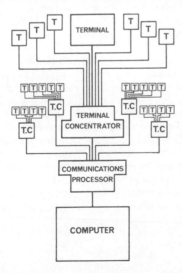

units especially if there is a large number of terminals of varying types on the network sending messages at different speeds and in different codes. Because of this a number of computer systems now connect all terminals into a *communications processor*. This is essentially a small purpose-built computer usually with its own memory whose job it is to control all the terminals attached to it, and pass their messages to and from the main computer which then doesn't have to worry about what type of terminal has sent a particular message or is to receive a message.

"As a matter of fact this approach has been taken one stage further in some large networks by the installation of *terminal concentrators* whose function is similar to a communications processor but which are located one step nearer the terminal. Hence in a large network possibly 40 concentrators, each with anything up to, say, 50 terminals connected, could themselves be connected through one communications processor to the main computer system.

"Incidentally," Rufus added, "I should tell you that if any unit — terminal or peripheral — is in electronic communication with the CPU we say that the unit is *on-line*."

How fast is fast

"You said earlier that computers, if not very bright, are at least fast," said Fred. "But how fast is fast?"

"Oh, very fast," replied Rufus. "For instance, a medium-speed CPU can add two numbers in a few millionths of a second. So it can perform 100,000 additions in a fraction of a second. If a human could add two numbers in one second it would take him over a day's continuous work to add 100,000 numbers in the same way. Data can be passed to and from magnetic discs at over 100,000,000 bytes a minute. Line printers can print 2000 lines (240,000 bytes) a minute."

"Yes," said Fred nodding his head gravely. "That is fast."

So fast, in fact, that a computer could read this whole book from magnetic discs in less time than you can read this line of print. With this sort of speed, then, it's very necessary to make sure that your computer is doing exactly what you want it to do otherwise as technology advances you will find that every improvement only enables you to make yet bigger mistakes even faster.

HOW TO WRITE A BASIC PROGRAM

or, Fred goes bi-lingual

"I've just written to a computer I know," remarked Fred nonchalantly, handing Rufus a neatly written letter, "asking it to solve a little problem I've got. Just check it for spelling please."

"The spelling's all right," said Rufus after skimming the contents. "But I can assure you, Fred, that's no way to talk to a computer."

"Should I perhaps have signed it 'yours very humbly'?" suggested Fred anxiously.

Dear Mr Computer,

I should very much like to know what is the largest rectangular area I can have if I am given a 100 metre rope that I can lay alongside a long wall so that part of the wall forms one side of my rectangle.

May I suggest that you call the length of each side at right angles to the wall x metres so that the area is $x \times (100 - 2x)$. Starting with x equal to 1 metre and increasing the length by steps of 1 metre until x is 50 metres find at each step the area formed. Then at the end you can tell me the largest area so formed together with the lengths of each side of the rectangle. Don't you think this is a good idea?

I hope you are well and have recovered from your blown fuse of yesterday.

Yours sincerely

Fred

"That won't help either. No, Fred, what you still haven't appreciated is that computers are very, very childlike. No computer could possibly understand what you've written. Like most very young children they have, in fact, an extremely limited vocabulary and it is essential that you don't go outside it."

"Limited vocabulary? You mean they only know a few words?"

"That's right."

"Very well. Tell me the words and I'll re-write my letter," said Fred taking out his pencil.

"Ah, now, that depends upon which language you want to use with your computer."

"Language? Why, English, of course. As a matter of fact it's all I know."

"No, no. I don't mean language in that sense. I mean *computer* language. You see, Fred, computer people have invented different languages or codes so that they can give their computers unambiguous and rigid instructions that designate the required operations and advise the addresses of the required data."

"Rufus," said Fred coldly, "you're talking nonense again."

"Oh, dear," sighed Rufus wearily. "I think the only thing to do is to teach you one of the languages. Then you'll appreciate better what it's all about. As it happens there's a language specially developed for people like you, Fred, who want to know how to give instructions to a computer without becoming sophisticated programmers. It's designed to be easy to use and remember and is called BASIC."

"Why BASIC?"

"Because that stands for Beginners All-purpose Symbolic Instruction Code — which is what it is."

It's all done with boxes.

"Now," began Rufus, "first you must appreciate that instructing a computer is rather like asking a well-intentioned but fundamentally obtuse person to carry out a given calculation. Though simple-minded, that person can add, subtract, multiply and divide very rapidly — the problem really being to ensure that he has the correct numbers to work with in the first place. The best way to envisage the solution to this problem is to imagine that there are lots and lots of boxes — each having its own identifying label. For instance, we could have six boxes labelled A, B, C, D, E, and F."

"But there aren't any boxes in a computer," protested Fred.

"No, but there are 'areas of memory' and I want you to regard such areas as being like these boxes. As you will appreciate, if you arrange to have a particular number in a given area of memory then this is equivalent to having that number in a given box."

"I'll go along with that," said Fred.

"Now we call the label on the box its *address* since it identifies in which box (or area of the memory) the required number is to be found. And instructing a computer can be likened to telling a little man who lives in the computer to put numbers in boxes and use numbers he finds in boxes. So if we told him to put '2' into box B, and then later to use the number in box B he'll use '2'. And if we then told him to put '4'

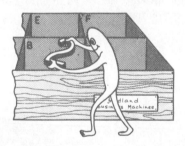

in box A and subsequently to multiply the numbers in boxes A and B and put the answer in box C we'd find at the end that '8' was in box C."

"If I don't actually ask the computer to tell me the number in box C," said Fred thoughtfully, "then I take it that although I don't know an '8' is there, any reference by me to box C will result in the little computer man using the '8'?"

"Exactly. So *addressing* box C, as we call such a reference, results in him using the number inside, the value of which may be totally unknown to you."

"How long a number can you put in a box?" asked Fred.

"That depends on the space in the memory allocated to each box — which in turn depends upon the design of the computer," replied Rufus. "But for practical purposes it's as long as any number you're likely to need."

Programming

"Next," continued Rufus, "I hope you appreciate that a computer has no opinion of its own. It must never, then, be asked anything but must only be given very firm instructions."

"I've heard people say they've asked their computer things," Fred argued. "And I'm sure it would be reasonable for me to ask one what 12345 x 54321 came to — if I needed such a calculation."

"It's a very loose way of talking," said Rufus severely. "What you'd actually do is to instruct the computer to multiply 12345 by 54321 and then print out the answer. No, Fred, you must always give your computer firm instructions. And, incidentally, a complete sequence of such instructions is called a *program*."

"I'd call it a liberty," muttered Fred. "But then I'm a creature with sensibilities."

"Computers can be difficult, too," replied Rufus. "If you deviate only fractionally from the correct code or program lay-out then they will refuse to do anything except perhaps snap back 'Illegal entry', or 'Invalid format', or, if they're feeling particularly unhelpful, just '???'."

"All right. So please explain to me just how to instruct these touchy servants so as to avoid upsetting them."

"Well, to start with in BASIC you must give *every instruction a number* so that by following the instructions one by one in number order the computer will, in fact, do exactly as you instruct. Next you must use the exact code word and punctuation."

"Punctuation?"

"Yes. In BASIC, for instance, you must never put a full stop in an instruction, and as for commas and semi-colons, well these are themselves code symbols having special meanings to the man in the computer. But more of that later. To start with, let's see how to put a number in a box."

LET, +,−,*,/, and PRINT

"Surely it's just a matter of saying something like 'put 2 in box B, isn't it?" asked Fred.

"Unfortunately not," replied Rufus. "Or fortunately not, for the BASIC code is even shorter. You merely write 'LET B = 2'. The word LET tells the computer man he must put in the box referred to immediately afterwards the number that follows the = sign."

"So LET A = 4 would have the effect of putting '4' in box 'A'?"

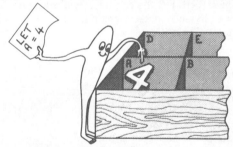

"It would. Now the arithmetic code. This simply involves the normal arithmetical signs except that * is used for multiplication (so as not to confuse our little man with the similarity between the letter X and the multiplication sign x) and / instead of ÷ for division. The code also includes other mathematical symbols such as = (equals), < (is less than), and > (is greater than)."

"So if I gave the instruction 2∗4 the man would multiply 2 by 4?"

"He would. But that's not enough in itself. You also need to tell him in the same instruction just what to do with the answer otherwise he will push it up the computer's wires and it will never be seen again."

"Put it in box C?" Fred suggested.

"In that case you'd write LET C = 2∗4."

"So he'll find the answer when he wants it in box C. How, though, can *I* look in box C myself?"

"If you put PRINT C the computer will print out the number that's in C. In fact, whatever you put after the word PRINT the computer will print."

Fred writes a program in practice

"Well, I'm learning," said Fred. "But I suppose it will be a long time yet before I can write a program myself."

"Nonsense," retorted Rufus. "You can write one now. Let's say I want the computer to put 4 and 2 into boxes A and B respectively, as it just did, then add the numbers in A and B and put the answer in C, and finally tell me what is in C. Write me the program."

With some trepidation Fred picked up his pencil and cautiously began to write his program. At the end he looked anxiously at Rufus.

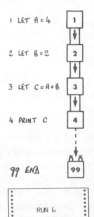

"Very good," commented Rufus. "I should, perhaps, warn you that many BASIC systems call for an END instruction. The reason, Fred, is that before actually carrying out any instructions at all the little man must set up all his computer units and memory ready. In effect, he first 'digests' the program. When you're feeding him the program, therefore, it is sometimes necessary to tell him the program is all complete and you haven't stopped giving him instructions merely because you haven't thought the next one out." And Rufus added '99 END' to Fred's program.

"But why '99'?" demanded Fred. "5's the next instruction number."

"It's a practical point," Rufus explained. "Your numbers don't have to run without a break. All the computer does is take the instructions in number order. If there are any gaps it just leaps over them."

"Perhaps it does, but why bother to leave them in the first place?"

"Because then you can insert additional instructions in between your other instructions without having to renumber the rest of the program — and when in practice you're trying to get a complicated program just right that could be very useful indeed."

"Just what would the computer produce if you gave it that program?" Fred asked curiously.

"Let's see," replied Rufus, and calling his secretary sent her off to the computer room with instructions to "run" their program.

Five minutes later she was back with the computer printout.

"Well, well, well," exclaimed Fred. "It's right first time."

Fred learns the difference between reading and removing

Next Fred asked a very sensible question. "Tell me," he said, "when the computer man uses a number from a box does that leave the box empty? I mean, after PRINT C is box C empty?"

"No," replied Rufus. "All the man does is *read* the number — not *remove* it; it stays there no matter how many times it's used."

"Can it ever be removed?"

"Oh, easily. A LET instruction will automatically remove whatever number was originally in the box and replace it with the number after the = sign. I might perhaps just add that in some systems a box with a zero in it is *not* empty — only a box with no symbol at all in it is empty."

"Talking of empty," said Fred, "I think it's lunch time."

Fred meets a longer program

"While you were at lunch," said Rufus that afternoon, "I took the opportunity to add some instructions to your program. Here it is — together with the resulting printout."

```
 1 LET A = 4
 2 LET B = 2
 3 LET C = A + B
 4 PRINT C

 5 LET C = A - B
 6 PRINT C
 7 PRINT A * B
 8 LET A = A + 1
 9 PRINT A
10 PRINT A + B * A - (A + B)
11 PRINT (A + B) * A - A + B
12 PRINT A/B * A
99 END
```

RUN	INSTRUCTION NUMBER
6	4
2	6
8	7
5	9
8	10
32	11
12.5	12

Fred carefully studied Rufus' program and printout.

"I notice," he remarked, pointing to instruction 7, "that PRINT can be followed by an actual calculation."

"Yes. As I said earlier, whatever you put after PRINT the computer will print — even the answer to a calculation," Rufus replied. "After all, if you don't want to keep the answer in the computer there's no point in allocating a box to it."

"Instruction 8 looks odd. I mean, how can A = A + 1?"

"We're not saying that. We're saying 'Take the number in box A (this being the A *after* the = sign), add 1 to it and put the answer in box A'."

"So the old number goes out of A and the new number, which is just one more, goes in — is that it?"

"You've got the idea," Rufus replied.

Fred returned to studying Rufus's program but had considerable difficulty checking how instruction 10 gave him a printout of '8', instruction 11 one of '32' and instruction 12 '12.5'. He wasn't able to make the check, in fact, until Rufus had explained that in a mixed calculation where addition, subtraction, multiplication and division were all carried out in the same instruction the computer followed self-imposed rules as regards the order in which the calculations were done.

After Rufus had explained these rules Fred was able to work out that instruction 10 gave him $5 + 2 \times 5 - (5 + 2) = 5 +$

RULES FOR MIXED CALCULATIONS

Calculation to be done on basis of following priorities:-

1) All calculations within brackets to be made

2) All multiplications and divisions to be made

3) All additions and subtractions to be made

If a calculation mixes multiplication and division, or addition and subtraction, then work from left to right.

$(2 \times 5) - 7 = 5 + 10 - 7 = 8$, instruction 11 gave him $(5 + 2) \times 5 - 5 + 2 = 7 \times 5 - 5 + 2 = 35 - 5 + 2 = 32$, and instruction 12 gave him $(5 \div 2) \times 5 = 2.5 \times 5 = 12.5$.

Fred does an IF — THEN and a GO TO

"So you can see, you can already write programs," Rufus pointed out. "Though not, as yet, *powerful* ones — that is, programs which enable difficult problems to be solved using only a few basic instructions. And the first of the instructions that builds up BASIC 'power' is the IF — THEN instruction. This tells the computer to proceed to a designated instruction should a stipulated condition hold."

"Eh?" blinked Fred.

"Well," explained Rufus. "I mean, if we had, say, IF B = 2 THEN 99 somewhere in the earlier program, then since B *does* equal 2 the computer at that point would leap to instruction 99 — which, as 99 is the end of the program, means that in this case the computer would stop."

"And if B didn't equal 2?"

"The computer would just pass to the next instruction in turn. Look, tell me what I'll get if I run this program," Rufus asked, drafting a short simple program.

Fred followed it through carefully.

"Since A does *not* equal B + 10," he asserted confidently, "the computer proceeds to instruction 4 and prints '111'."

"Excellent, Fred," congratulated Rufus. "Now meet an even simpler instruction — GO TO. This simply tells the computer to go to a designated

1 LET A = 4

2 LET B = 2

3 IF A = B + 10
   THEN 99

4 PRINT 111

99 END

RUN
111

destination. For example, GO TO 99 anywhere in any of our earlier programs would have sent the computer straight to the end."

"And that should win the prize for the most useless instruction ever invented," sniffed Fred.

"On the contrary. Used intelligently it is one of the most valuable. To take a simple example, what if in our last program I had wanted '222' to be printed if A *did* happen to equal B + 10 instead of the 111 that would be printed if it didn't? How would you amend it?"

Fred thought for a moment and then added '5 PRINT 222' and at the same time changed the '99' in instruction 3 to '5'. Rufus took the program without a word and ran it. Fred stared in amazement at the 222 on the printout.

"Now why in heaven's name did it print '222' when without a shadow of a doubt. A does *not* equal B + 10?" he asked plaintively.

"Because, rightly, it ignored the jump to instruction 5 at the IF — THEN instruction, proceeded to instruction 4 and then, since it was next in turn, passed on to and obeyed instruction 5."

"But how can I stop it proceeding to the next instruction?" wailed Fred.

"By simply writing GO TO 99 between instructions 4 and 5. It means renumbering your program to fit it in, though, I'm afraid."

It took Rufus but a moment to

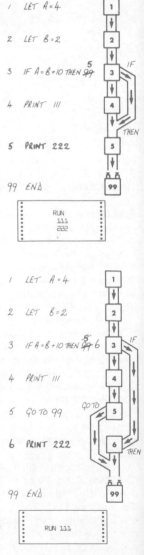

produce the amended program which Fred had to admit filled the bill exactly.

Fred learns to loop

"Probably the most powerful programming technique," said Rufus, "is inserting an instruction that sends the computer *back* up the program. Say you started with the number '1', kept doubling up and wanted to know how many times you'd need to double up to reach 1048576. Do you agree that this would give you your answer?"

Fred worked carefully through the program Rufus handed to him.

"You're going up in instruction steps of 10," Fred observed. "I take it that's to avoid the sort of difficulty we had when we amended the last program."

```
10  LET N = 0
20  LET A = 1
30  LET N = N+1
40  LET A = 2*A
50  IF A = 1048576
    THEN 70
60  GO TO 30
70  PRINT N
99  END
```

```
RUN 20
```

"It is. You'll notice, by the way, that I've started the whole thing off by saying in instruction 10 that where there has been *no* doubling up then (in instruction 20) A will be 1."

"Yes, and after increasing N to 1 in instruction 30 you've then written the program in such a way that every time A (which instruction 40 doubles up) fails to equal 1048576 in instruction 50, instruction 60 sends the computer back to instruction 30 where N is increased by 1. So N is, in fact, keeping count of the number of times A is doubled. Once 1048576 is reached the IF — THEN of instruction 50 takes the computer down to instruction 70 where it prints the current value of N and then stops."

"Yes. Very good. And instructions 30 to 60 form what we call a *loop* — that is, a part of the program where the computer goes round and round until it is taken out of the loop by some condition being fulfilled in an IF — THEN instruction."

For interest Rufus then ran the program and Fred saw that N reached 20.

"You must have known that doubling up would eventually

give 1048576," remarked Fred thoughtfully. "But what would happen if you'd put in, say 1048577 by mistake?"

"Well, since A would never come to equal 1048577 the computer would never break out of the loop. It would keep going round the loop forever — or until somebody stopped the computer. We'd have, in fact, what is called an *endless loop.*"

"I think I've something like that when it comes to weeding my garden," grumbled Fred.

Fred meets READ and DATA

"I must say," complained Fred after he'd tried writing a few programs on his own, "this LET business gets very long-winded when I've a whole string of numbers to put into the program."

"Ah, well, we do have two special instructions to cater for that problem," Rufus replied. "These are READ and DATA. The idea here is to list after the instruction READ all the boxes you wish to fill (with commas between box addresses to tell the man when he has come to the end of an address) and after the instruction DATA write all the numbers you wish to put into those boxes (with commas between numbers). Now the important thing to grasp about the DATA instruction is that as the computer makes its 'digestion' run through the program (which, as I've explained, it does *before* carrying out any of the instructions *including* READ) *it queues up these numbers as if they were at a taxi rank* — and there they stay until the program is actually run and a READ instruction is reached. Then the first number *leaves the queue* and goes into the first box address given in the READ instruction, the next number going into the next box and so on until all the boxes given in the READ instruction have been filled. If this doesn't clear the queue the remaining numbers patiently wait queued up until another READ provides more boxes."

"So I take it that every time the computer comes to a READ instruction it puts the next numbers in the queue into the box addresses given. Well, that means 'READ A, B, C' and DATA 66, 77, 88' will result in 66 going into box A, 77 into B and 88 into C."

"Exactly."

"But I'm not really sure how it works if the first READ instruction doesn't clear the queue."

"Well, look here," replied Rufus quickly listing and running a simple program. "As you can see, the computer has picked up and added, as requested, each pair of numbers in turn."

"So in effect we've got four calculations for the price of one program," observed Fred. "That's handy. But as a matter of interest doesn't that program have an endless loop?"

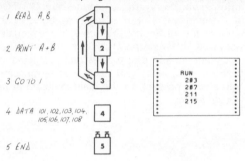

```
1  READ A,B

2  PRINT A+B

3  GO TO 1

4  DATA 101,102,103,104,
        105,106,107,108

5  END
```

```
RUN
 203
 207
 211
 215
```

"Well, yes, from a logical point of view it does. However, on the fifth time round the computer finds there are no numbers left waiting in the queue to be read despite the fact it has more boxes for them. So it has to stop — telling you in some systems that it has run out of data to read as required by instruction 1."

"Whereabouts in the program do you put your DATA instructions?"

"Anywhere you want. All a computer does when it comes to DATA during its 'digestion' phase is to queue up the numbers given — behind any old numbers from an earlier DATA instruction if need be."

Fred does a GOSUB and RETURN

"I must just explain to you one other useful pair of instructions," said Rufus. "It often happens that in a long program you require exactly the same calculation to be made at different places using different figures. For example, in a program involving interest on money it may be necessary on a number of occasions to find out how many days there are between two given dates. Because of the different lengths of the months this calculation can require a rather longish 'mini' program. However, rather than write out the whole of this program at each point

in the main program you can write it just once and there-
after instruct the computer to carry out that particular part of
the program each time the calculation is needed. Such a 'mini'
program is called a *subroutine*, and using subroutines, as you
can imagine, can save considerable programming time."

"Well, I don't see the need for any new instruction. Surely
you can bring in your subroutines just by using GO TOs?"

"Bring them in yes — but it's getting back to the main
program that's the difficulty. You see, since you leave the
main program at different points you need to get back to it
at different points — and that creates real problems in ending
your subroutine. No, what you need is an arrangement that
ensures you always go back to the main program *at the point
you previously left it.*"

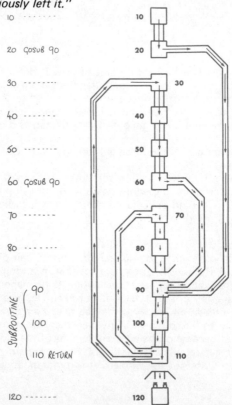

"And how do you achieve this admirable objective?" asked Fred.

"Well, you write your subroutine as part of the total program, putting as your last instruction 'RETURN'. After this, each time you want to use the subroutine you just write GOSUB followed by the number of first instruction in the subroutine. This acts as a GO TO. Then when the computer reaches RETURN it will automatically go back to join the main program at the very point it left it to carry out the subroutine."

How to persuade your computer to write English

"The wonders of modern science," grinned Fred. "But one thing still bothers me. I can get the computer to print out a whole string of numbers, but unless I can remember just how I wrote my program I won't know what each number refers to."

"No problem," replied Rufus. "All you need to do is to insert in the PRINT instruction a short English statement *between quotes* which will make reference to the answer the computer is printing out. For example, if your computer is going to print out a required total which is held in, say, box Z, you'd write PRINT "THE REQUIRED TOTAL IS"; Z. I should point out to you that *everything* lying between the quotes will be reproduced on the printout and that by putting a semicolon between the last quote and your box number you instruct the computer to print the contents of Z at the end of the quoted phrase."

"That seems eminently simple," said Fred.

REM, INPUT, STOP and FOR—NEXT

There are a number of other BASIC instructions (particularly in respect of arranging the presentation of the printout — though this aspect of programming is ignored here) of which perhaps four may have interest for us now. These are:

* REM (short for REMark). This is not strictly an instruction at all and is ignored by the computer when running the program. Its function is merely to explain to anybody looking at the program just what at that point the program is all about.

* INPUT. On reaching this instruction the computer prints out a "?" and waits until the operator inserts a figure or

series of figures. It is a form of READ instruction where the data is inserted *during* the program run.

* STOP. This instruction simply stops the computer without needing to send it to the END instruction.

* FOR — NEXT. This is a loop instruction that sends the computer a designated number of times round a loop before it can continue with the rest of the program. The FOR part of the instruction marks the beginning of the loop and also specifies how many loops are to be made, and the NEXT part of the instruction marks the end of the loop (and sends the computer back up to the FOR instructions unless it happens to be the last loop). For instance, FOR N = 1 TO 6 will result in the computer looping six times, i.e. each time it reaches the instruction NEXT N, setting N at 1, 2, 3, 4, 5 and 6 respectively for each loop — after which it will proceed to the instruction that follows the NEXT N instruction.

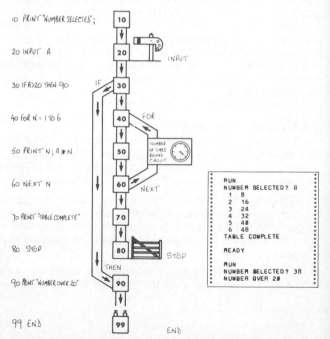

```
1.  REM THIS PROGRAM GIVES THE MULTIPLICATION TABLE FOR
    ANY SELECTED NUMBER, NOT OVER 20, FROM 1 TO 6 TIMES

10  PRINT "NUMBER SELECTED";          10

20  INPUT A                           20        INPUT

30  IF A>20 THEN 90           IF      30

40  FOR N = 1 TO 6                    40        FOR

50  PRINT N; A * N                    50        NUMBER OF TIMES ROUND CIRCUIT

60  NEXT N                            60        NEXT

70  PRINT "TABLE COMPLETE"            70

80  STOP                              80        STOP

90  PRINT "NUMBER OVER 20"    THEN    90

99  END                               99        END
```

```
RUN
NUMBER SELECTED? 8
  1    8
  2   16
  3   24
  4   32
  5   40
  6   48
TABLE COMPLETE

READY

RUN
NUMBER SELECTED? 38
NUMBER OVER 20
```

Finally, it should perhaps be mentioned that any instruction that may lead to the computer jumping forwards or backwards instead of moving to the next instruction in sequence (*e.g.* GO TO, IF – THEN, GOSUB, FOR – NEXT) is called a *branching* instruction.

Fred gets his answer

"Now let's see you write a *proper* letter to your computer," suggested Rufus. "One that will enable it to solve your rope and area problem for you."

Fred thought this an excellent idea. It took him a little while to write his program — and even longer to get it correct so that it would give him the answer he wanted (a process that Rufus explained was called *debugging*). But he succeeded in the end, and after running the program he and Rufus studied the resulting printout.

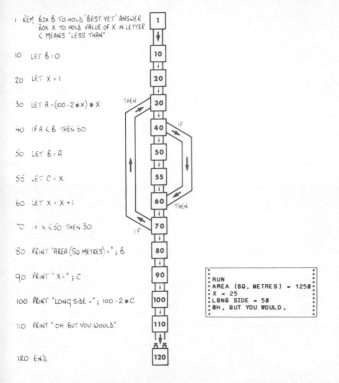

```
 1  REM  BOX B TO HOLD 'BEST YET' ANSWER
        BOX X TO HOLD VALUE OF X IN LETTER
        < MEANS "LESS THAN"

10  LET B = 0

20  LET X = 1

30  LET A = (100 - 2 * X) * X

40  IF A < B THEN 60

50  LET B = A

55  LET C = X

60  LET X = X + 1

70  IF X < 50 THEN 30

80  PRINT "AREA (SQ METRES) = "; B

90  PRINT " X = "; C

100 PRINT "LONG SIDE = "; 100 - 2 * C

110 PRINT " OH BUT YOU WOULD"

120 END
```

```
RUN
AREA (SQ. METRES) = 1250
X = 25
LONG SIDE = 50
OH, BUT YOU WOULD.
```

"Of course I would have solved this problem a different way — using differential calculus instead of bothering the computer," Rufus remarked pompously. "By the way, what's this 'OH BUT YOU WOULD'?"

"Just the retort the computer and I wished to make when you said *you'd* do it a different way — which, from experience, I knew you would," replied Fred.

SOME BASIC MEANINGS

CODE	MEANING	CODE	MEANING
LET	Put into	DATA	Put given data in data list queue
+	Add	GOSUB	Go to designated Subroutine
−	Subtract	RETURN	Return from Subroutine to previous point in main program
*	Multiply		
/	Divide	INPUT	Operator to insert data for entry into designated box
PRINT	Print out		
END	End of Program	FOR · NEXT	FOR given number of times loop program at NEXT instruction
IF·THEN	IF stipulated condition holds THEN proceed to designated instruction		
		STOP	Stop
GOTO	Go to designated instruction	" "	Print out everything between quotes
READ	Put next piece of data in designated box		

Fred has just written the four programs below. Do you think he will get the printout he wants in each case? If there are any you have doubts about, can you say where he went wrong?

Program 1
```
1 REM THIS PROGRAM PRINTS
  THE NUMBERS FROM 1 TO 10.
10 LET N = 1
20 PRINT N
30 LET N = N+1
40 IF N = 10 THEN 60
50 GO TO 20
60 END
```

Program 2
```
1 REM THIS PROGRAM PRINTS
  THE CUMULATIVE TOTALS
  FORMED BY PROGRESSIVELY
  ADDING ALL THE NUMBERS
  FROM 1 TO 10.
10 FOR N = 1 TO 10
20 READ A
30 LET T = T+A
40 PRINT "CUMULATIVE
  TOTALS =";T
50 NEXT A
60 DATA 1,2,3,4,5,6,7,8,9,10
70 END
```

Program 3
```
1 REM THIS PROGRAM DETER-
  MINES THE VALUE N MUST
  TAKE IN ORDER THAT 5✻N
  = 30.
10 READ A, B, N
20 LET N = N+1
30 LET A = A✻N
40 IF B = A THEN 60
50 GO TO 20
60 PRINT N
70 DATA 5, 30, 0
80 END
```

Program 4
```
1 REM IF 6 NUMBERS ARE
  SELECTED THEN THIS PRO-
  GRAM WILL IDENTIFY ANY
  NUMBER WHICH MAY HAPPEN
  TO BE DUPLICATED (THIS
  ASSUMES NO MORE THAN A
  SINGLE DUPLICATION).
2 REM ON "?" IN PRINTOUT
  INSERT GIVEN 6 NUMBERS.
5 INPUT A, B, C, D, E, F
10 PRINT "THE DUPLICATED
  NUMBER IS —";
20 IF A = B THEN 170
30 IF A = C THEN 170
40 IF A = D THEN 170
50 IF A = E THEN 170
60 IF A = F THEN 170
70 IF B = C THEN 190
80 IF B = D THEN 190
90 IF B = E THEN 190
100 IF B = F THEN 190
110 IF C = D THEN 210
120 IF C = E THEN 210
130 IF C = F THEN 210
140 IF D = E THEN 230
150 IF D = F THEN 230
160 IF E = F THEN 250
170 PRINT A
180 STOP
190 PRINT B
200 STOP
210 PRINT C
220 STOP
230 PRINT D
240 STOP
250 PRINT E
260 END
```

ANSWERS OVERLEAF

ANSWERS

I. Instruction 40 sends program to end *before* "10" is printed.

   TO CORRECT: Re-write as 40 ... IF N = 11 THEN 60

II. It is N, not A, that is the subject of the FOR ... NEXT instructions, so instruction 50 is wrong.

   TO CORRECT: Re-write as 50 ... NEXT N

   Also as it stands the program will result in "CUMULATIVE TOTALS" being printed every time a cumulative total is printed — which, while not perhaps wrong, is inelegant.

   TO CORRECT: Add instruction 5 ... PRINT "CUMULATIVE TOTALS =";
   Re-write instruction 40 as 40 ... PRINT T;

III. This will give the answer "3". Fred failed to realise that instruction 30 uses the "A" of the *previous loop* instead of "5".

   TO CORRECT: Re-write instruction 30 as 30 ... LET A = 5*N

IV. If there is *no* duplicated number this program will print out the first number in the INPUT instruction as the duplicated number. This is because Fred failed to notice that if none of his IF — THEN instructions involved a duplicated number after instruction 160 the computer would pass as a matter of course to instruction 170 and print number in address A.

   TO CORRECT: Add instructions 165 ... PRINT "THERE IS NO DUPLICATED NUMBER."
   166 ... STOP

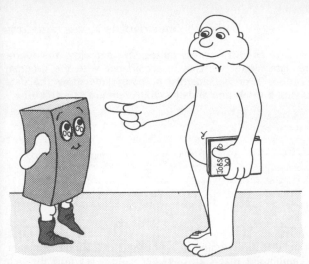

4. HOW YOU GIVE ORDERS TO THE COMPUTER

"Now, Rufus," said Fred the next day, "not so very long ago you said that there was no little man in the computer. Yet yesterday all you did was talk about such a little man. Come, now, admit it — there *is* somebody inside the CPU."

"Well, I suppose I must plead guilty to the indictment of expounding on the technique of programming in anthropomorphic terms," replied Rufus apologetically. "Perhaps, then, before we go any further I'd better try and show you how a computer's wires, switches and electrical pulses can have an understanding of plain English."

Data circuitry and control circuitry

"The first thing you need to appreciate," began Rufus, "is that there are two quite different kinds of circuitry in a computer. First, there is the *data circuitry*. This is the circuitry that carries the pulses which represent actual data — such as your rope length in yesterday's little problem. These pulses obviously need to go in and out of the data addresses and also through the various arithmetical parts of the CPU. But, of course, they can't be left to run berserk through the circuit — their movements must be guided and controlled by switches in that circuit. And this brings us to the second type of circuitry,

the *control circuitry*, whose pulses open and close the appropriate data circuit switches in accordance with the program
instructions. For explanatory purposes let's show the data
circuit as a thick line and the control circuit as a thin line,"

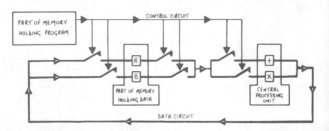

continued Rufus sketching a brief diagram. "I should, incidentally, emphasise that control pulses cannot get into the data
circuitry nor data pulses into the control circuitry."

"All the control circuit lines end up at switches," Fred
observed.

"Yes. And when a pulse flows down the control circuit wire
to a given switch, it closes it, enabling data pulses to flow
through that switch. Note that in my diagram the data pulses
can only flow one way, clockwise, around the data circuitry.
Not that computers necessarily operate in precisely this way,"
added Rufus hastily. "But it will enable you to see, albeit
crudely, the manner in which instruction pulses enable data
pulses to be processed."

"Never mind the technical qualifications," said Fred gener-
ously. "What's next?"

"Well, next I'd like you to meet the NOT gate," replied
Rufus. "This is a gate of the kind we looked at when we
discussed how the computer work-
ed. This gate, which sits across but
a single wire, has the feature that
if a pulse arrives at the gate (where,
of course, it dies) no pulse departs
from the gate, while if *no pulse
arrives* during the beat of the
computer's internal clock then a
pulse is dispatched."

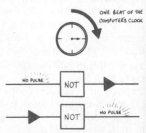

"Contrary sort of gate," murmured Fred.

"It is, rather. Now for simplicity let's assume that our computer uses 4-bit bytes rather than 8-bit — that is, there are four wires along which the pulses travel. These are in parallel, which means that each byte in a program instruction emerging from that part of the memory that holds the program travels along and then down *all* the control circuit wires leading to the data circuit switches."

"That would switch just about everything on, wouldn't it? Seems a nice recipe for chaos, if you ask me."

"You've obviously grasped the point — at least, as far as I've yet developed it. However, next let's arrange things so that just before the pulses reach a given switch they have to pass through a sequence of AND gates — firstly two across the left-hand and right-hand pairs of wires and secondly one across the two subsequent wires."

"In that case," said Fred thoughtfully, "the only byte which would result in a pulse reaching and travelling down the final wire after the last AND gate would be the byte that called for a pulse on every one of the four wires above, which is 1111. But such a byte will result in a pulse reaching all the gates. That's no improvement on the previous set up."

"No it's not. But what if we now start placing NOT gates before the AND gate sequences? Imagine, say, we take five sets of four such wires. We leave the first set as it is, but put NOT gates across other wires as I have drawn them. Then we send the byte 1011 down the whole five sets. Tell me, what will happen?"

Fred studied the wiring diagram carefully.

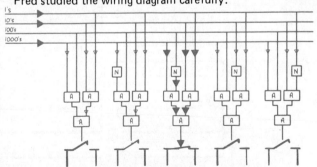

"Well," he said slowly, "since one wire of the four has no pulse it means that unless that wire passes through a NOT gate then it's impossible for all four wires to arrive at an AND gate sequence with pulses. So the only data circuit switch that can be closed by 1011 is the one where the set of control wires above it has a NOT gate across the second wire -- and in this case that's the middle set."

"Well done, Fred."

"And doesn't it follow that the particular data switch can be closed by *only* 1011 and no other byte?"

"It certainly does. And the point I'm making, Fred, is that by using our AND gate sequence in conjunction with different patterns of NOT gates in front of it then, despite the fact that an instruction byte travels down *all the wires* towards the data switches, only the set of wires that have a NOT gate pattern that exactly complements the byte pulses allows a pulse to pass through to the data switch."

"It's rather like locks and keys, isn't it? And I suppose you can build a NOT gate pattern that will match any given possible pulse arrangement?"

"You most definitely can. And that means that every different byte arrangements is able to close its own unique switch in the data circuit," said Rufus.

"And at the same time is blocked off from every other switch in the system. Very neat — very neat indeed."

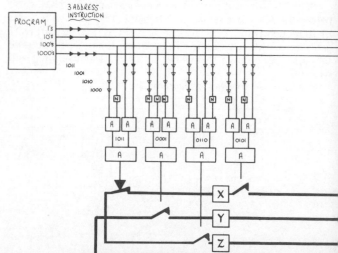

It's all done with pulses

"But I still don't see," complained Fred, "how this can result in an instruction such as LET X = Y + Z actually happening."

"That's the last step," replied Rufus. "As you'll no doubt appreciate, the majority of simple instructions require you to take two pieces of data out of their boxes, 'operate' on them, and then put the answer back in another box. Now such an instruction can be made up of four bytes — the first 'telling' the CPU what operation is to be done (and which is called the *function code*), and the next two 'telling' the computer the addresses where the two pieces of required data are to be found and the last 'telling' the computer where to put the answer. Such an instruction is called a *3-address instruction* and is useful to us here to illustrate how it is all done with pulses."

Fred settled himself down with an air of close attention.

"Now let's assume," Rufus went on, "that the function code for adding is 1000, that the codes to release the data from addresses Y and Z are 1010 and 1001 respectively, and that the code to insert data into address X is 1011. The 3-address instruction needed to perform LET X = Y + Z is, therefore, 1000, 1010, 1001, 1011. So out along the control wires run these four bytes."

"Ah," said Fred sitting up with interest. "Won't that mean that when the first byte 1000 runs down the wires to the data switches only the switch associated with 1000 will close?"

"It will. And that switch is, of course, the switch in the wire leading to the adding function in the CPU."

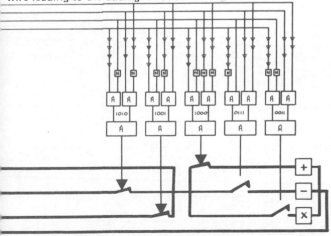

"Then, I suppose, when the next two bytes come down, they'll close the switches that let out the numbers in boxes Y and Z, and when the last byte comes down it closes the switch leading to box X."

"Exactly," confirmed Rufus. "So the whole instruction will result in all four appropriate switches being closed – after which the contents of Y and Z run along the data circuit into the adding part of the CPU and the answer runs round and into box X."

"Ah, Rufus," sighed Fred as he contemplated the inevitability by which the control pulses produced the desired result, "you've made my little man redundant. But look," he added suddenly, "isn't our little man necessary for deciding which instructions need to go out along the control circuitry?"

"Of course not. The instructions are simply stored in consecutive addresses (boxes, if you like) in the memory in the same sequence as they are written in the program. All that has to happen, then, is for these instructions to emerge one after the other in order."

"But what if there's a branching instruction?"

"It complicates things, admittedly. Yet essentially that involves no more than arranging for a different 'box' than the next to be switched into the sequence."

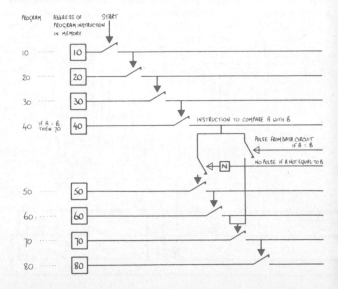

"Which I suppose, still only requires organising a few appropriate pulses," said Fred, idly sketching the idea of how an IF — THEN instruction could be obeyed within the memory. "But even so, how the devil does LET X = Y + Z become the pulse patterns 1000, 1010, 1001, 1011? Won't we need our little man to make the conversion?"

" *'Translation'* is the correct word," replied Rufus. "But your question is very pertinent and that's the next topic we must discuss. First, though, since we've come to a natural break in our discourse I suggest we take a little time off for a coffee or something, mmm?"

"I'd rather have a coffee," said Fred meekly.

The machine code — the only language the computer knows

"Now, Fred," said Rufus when they'd returned from the University bar, "what we have to look at next is this business you've raised of turning LET X = Y + Z into 1000, 1010, 1011. First, though, let me say that there's no need to give the computer its instructions in the 0 and 1 binary pattern form since all computer input devices are built with the ability to create the appropriate binary pulse patterns directly from ordinary numbers. Now in ordinary numbers the binary pulse form 1000 is 8, 1010 is 10, 1001 is 9 and 1011 is 11. So if we want the pulse pattern 1000, 1010, 1001, 1011 to emerge from the program memory we need only input the code 8, 10, 9, 11 to achieve this result — the computer automatically making the translation. And when we write our program in this form we say we are using *machine code* since this is the code (and, in fact, the only code) that the machine understands. So now you can see what a program written in machine code would look like. . . ."

"Oh, my goodness," exclaimed Fred. "I wouldn't fancy writing a long program in machine code."

"It's not fun, certainly. It means memorising all the function codes and then as the program develops keeping very close track on just what data is in each address."

"It would drive me crazy," muttered Fred.

"It did rather tend to have that result among the early programmers. But since the machine code is the only language a computer understands, at first they had no choice."

Fred meets an assembler

"You say 'at first'. You mean there was a way round it?"

"Yes — by developing other languages," replied Rufus. "But the whole subject of intermediate languages is confusing, Fred, and probably your best chance of grasping the operations and inter-relationships is for you to envisage yourself as a chef about to prepare a meal. You have to help a very obedient and fast-working assistant who unfortunately, though, has to be told every step he must take — and told in numbers, too."

"In numbers?"

"Yes. You see, a machine code is the only language he understands. Imagine, Fred you have in your culinary repertoire a recipe for steak and kidney pudding. You'll appreciate that giving your instructions to your assistant is essentially a matter of programming him and so in order to be a good chef you'll need to be a competent programmer."

"So I'll have to know the machine code, will I?"

"Well, it will be written up on the wall for you. Even so, giving each step-by-step instruction will be a rather lengthy business."

"I'd not only go crazy," Fred growled, "but everyone else would go hungry, too, that's for sure. But if my assistant only understands the machine code what's the alternative?"

"Well, to start with you could write out your program in mnemonic form after which all that would be necessary would be to translate the mnemonic code into machine code."

"Can't see that that's any improvement," said Fred emphatically. "I'd still have to write out the whole confounded thing in numbers."

"On the face of it I'll admit your criticism," Rufus conceded. "But think, Fred — a straight symbol-for-symbol translation from one code to another is an operation that merely calls for a strict following of a simple, if long, set of rules. And that's *just the sort of job at which the computer excels.*"

"Are you trying to tell me," demanded Fred slowly, "that I can get my computer to do the translation for me? That, in fact, I can get a computer to write out a program for itself it can understand by feeding it a program that it can't understand?"

"I am indeed. But what's surprising about that? If I were to say to you 'Drunk mad smiler snows' you'd be lost, but if I said re-write this ignoring the first and last letter of each

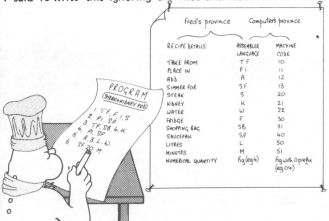

RECIPE DETAILS	ASSEMBLER LANGUAGE	MACHINE CODE
TAKE FROM	T F	10
PLACE IN	P I	11
ADD	A	12
SIMMER FOR	S F	13
STEAK	S	20
KIDNEY	K	21
WATER	W	22
FRIDGE	F	30
SHOPPING BAG	SB	31
SAUCEPAN	SP	40
LITRES	L	50
MINUTES	M	51
NUMERICAL QUANTITY	fig (eg 4)	fig with 0 prefix (eg 04)

fred's province   Computer's province

PROGRAM
(STEAK+KIDNEY PUD)

1. T.F. F. I. S
2. P I. SP
3. TF. SB. 4. K
4. P I. SP
5. A. 3. L. W
6. SF. 20. M

word you'd understand the instruction immediately — even if you couldn't carry it out," Rufus added eyeing Fred's figure.

"But won't we have to give the computer the translation rules first?" asked Fred, feeling Rufus's challenge was one best ignored.

"Well, naturally. We do, in fact, have to prepare a translation program written in machine code which is called an *assembler*. But once it's written it's there for always. All programs can then be written out in the mnemonic form I've already suggested — which is called the *assembler language* — and put into the computer in that form along with the assembler (a process known as *assembling*). Then out will come the whole program re-written in machine code either on punched cards, tape or disc storage."

"Which you just feed into the computer every time you want to run the program," broke in Fred. "Why, that's marvellous."

Higher and higher languages

"Don't let your enthusiasm run away with you," remonstrated Rufus. "Programming in assembler language is still a long, slow process since the need to detail every step for the machine code means a great deal of repetitive writing to take care of frequently recurring procedures — such as making steak and kidney puddings in cooking and finding square roots in business."

Fred looked hard at Rufus.

"You're not going to tell me, are you," he asked incredulously, "that programmers next invented an even simpler language that could be translated into assembler language — using the computer again?" he added sarcastically.

"Why not?"

"So that will mean we'll have a language which translates to a language which translates to a language which the computer will understand. Oh, my poor head," moaned Fred.

"Yes, it is a little confusing at first," admitted Rufus. "But to help clarify the matter we classify languages in terms of three levels. At the very bottom are the machine codes, and the ones above that, the assembler languages, we call the *low-level languages*. At the top we have the *high-level languages* which are translated to low-level languages using the same approach as that used in translating from a low-level language to a machine code. And high-level languages differ primarily from low-level languages by their ability to combine a number of low-level instructions into a single high-level instruction. So as a chef using a high-level language you could simply write something like SIMMER STEAK AND KIDS — which would be translated to the first six instructions of your assembler language program. So writing in a high-level language is the equivalent of writing out a whole recipe in terms of the main culinary steps."

"This rather suggests that for every high-level main step I'll need to have a low-level sequence of menial operations."

"Yes, indeed, Fred. And translating from a high-level to a low-level language involves preparing a further translation program that details for the computer the low-level operation-sequence called for by any given high-level language coding. Such a program is referred to as a *compiler*, and making the translation is termed *'compiling'*."

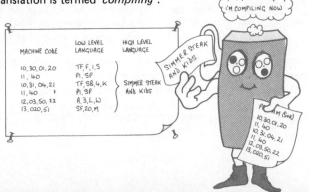

"So the compiler translates from high to low level and then hands over the result to the assembler for translation to machine code."

"Well, the double step is not really necessary since it's possible to design a compiler that translates straight into machine code."

"Yes, I suppose it is," said Fred after giving the matter a little thought. "After which, of course, you can feed the machine-coded program back into the computer and get it to make the steak and kidney pud — which was the whole object of the exercise. But tell me, Rufus, what if the high-level programmer makes a mistake in writing his program — say he writes SIMMER STEAK AND YOUNG GOATS. Won't that really throw a spanner in the works?"

"Oh, no. Before a computer translates any problem into

machine code it checks it thoroughly for such errors. This check is called a *syntax check* since essentially it is checking to see that the high-level program is what you might call grammatically correct. When it comes to a 'grammatical' error — where the programmer has written something that isn't part of the language or allowable under the language (coding) rules or isn't a specified term — the computer tells him what and where the error is. He can then correct it before going any further."

"I can see this high-level language stuff would save me the devil of a lot of work if I were a programmer, but I hate to think of writing the compiler," shuddered Fred. "That must be a real headache."

"It is certainly a rather arduous and lengthy task," Rufus agreed. "But you don't have to do that. It comes as part of the software that is supplied by the computer manufacturers."

"Thank goodness for that," said Fred with a sigh of relief. Then his face fell a little. "But hold on — a steak and kidney pud is just one dish in a meal. So if I want to write programs for whole meals it will mean that every time I want to include a steak and kidney pud I'll have to write out the whole steak and kidney pudding program. Even if I can do that in high-level language it will still mean a lot of work."

"Not necessarily. In such a case you'd only need to write out the steak and kidney pudding program once. This program you'd then designate *subroutine* (of the kind we met when we discussed BASIC), give it a code name (such as 'STEAK & KIDNEY PUD') and put it in your subroutine library — which involves no more than having the computer write the program on tape or disc specially allocated to the task of holding your subroutines. Then, when you want to incorporate the sub-routine in your main program, you just write the code name at

the appropriate place in your main program and the compiler will automatically look up this code name in the library and slot it into the machine code program."

"I'm getting the impression," said Fred severely, "that programming is a very, very feather-bedded profession."

Babel Unlimited — the language shop

"That apart," continued Fred, "I think now that I'm ready to learn this high-level language of yours."

"Ah, but, you see, there's more than one," said Rufus.

"More than one?" Fred blinked. "Don't see the point of that. Who wants to learn a whole load of languages?"

"Well, different requirements call for different high-level words. Take your cooking, for example. A word you'd need very frequently would be BAKE but computers in business would probably never have any cause to use the word at all."

"You're suggesting different languages are invented for different needs, are you?" asked Fred and when Rufus nodded continued, "All right, just what languages are there, then?"

"I think my best answer to that," replied Rufus, "is to take you to the Language Shop."

In the Language Shop Rufus waved towards the counters that stood facing Fred.

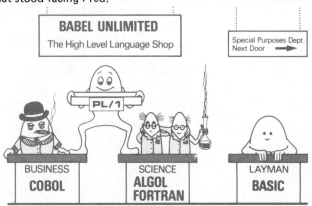

"These languages have all been developed with the object of being employed *generally* in the major fields of computer applications," he explained. "So we have business served by COBOL, science by ALGOL and FORTRAN, and the layman by BASIC."

"But I know BASIC!"

"Yes. I taught you BASIC because it was designed as a simple-to-learn language which would enable non-computer minded individuals to write and run their own programs. But BASIC isn't much use to you if you have large amounts of data or a highly complex number problem."

"Why do we seem to have two languages on the Science counter?" Fred asked.

"Historical, really. Both ALGOL and FORTRAN serve much the same needs but were developed independently. Both have the feature of providing almost everything in the mathematical world. For instance, if you want a square root in FORTRAN you just write SQRT and the compiler will incorporate into the machine code program the procedure for extracting a square root. Similarly SIN and COS result in the compiler incorporating sine and cosine procedures."

"Just as my SIMMER STEAK AND KIDS would lead to the full procedure being slotted into my own program, I suppose."

"That's right. So for scientific applications these two languages are fine. However, they have very little to offer when it comes to handling large quantities of data. Then COBOL serves best — though conversely it has very little in the way of scientific words."

"And what on earth is all that up in the air?" asked Fred viewing the rather acrobatic counter-assistant's antics with considerable curiosity.

"You mean PL/1? Well, that's an attempt to provide a language that caters for both business and science under a single umbrella language. It has facilities for both mathematical functions and large data masses."

"That should make COBOL, ALGOL and FORTRAN redundant."

"Not altogether. Certainly the fewer the languages there are the less difficulties computer manufacturers have designing their hardware and software to cope with languages. On the other hand, as you know, Fred, on the whole the more general purpose a thing is the less suitable it usually is for a specific application. Your GP knows something about every ailment but probably wouldn't be as good at treating a foot complaint as a chiropodist."

"So what you're saying, are you, is that if my sole interest is in business — which it is at the moment — then PL/1 wouldn't really fit me as well as COBOL?"

"Yes."

"Right, then. In that case you'd better tell me a bit more about COBOL," said Fred.

COBOL — a common business orientated language

"COBOL (from **CO**mmon **B**usiness **O**rientated **L**anguage)," began Rufus, "is a language specifically designed to cope with business data and procedures. One of its main features is the extent to which program instructions look like ordinary English statements."

"Example, example," demanded Fred.

"Well, MULTIPLY PRICE-PER-UNIT BY NUMBER-OF-UNITS GIVING SALES-VALUE is a COBOL instruction — the compiler recognising MULTIPLY . . . BY as the function code, PRICE-PER-UNIT and NUMBER-OF-UNITS as the addresses of the data to be operated upon, and SALES-VALUE as the address of the answer."

"Funny addresses."

"Yes, but very meaningful. And even the subroutines themselves have names instead of numbers so that a GO TO . . . instruction in COBOL could read PERFORM SALES-VALUE-CALCULATION where SALES-VALUE-CALCULATION would be the name of the required subroutine."

"I like that," said Fred. "Can you use whatever groups of words you want for addresses and subroutines?"

"Yes, though there are a limited number of words you *can't* use. These are called *reserved words* and by and large they relate to function code words. I mean, you obviously can't have MULTIPLY as a function code *and* as an address or subroutine name so its use is forbidden in the latter two forms. Other than that you can use whatever words you wish — providing, incidentally, that you put a hyphen between the ordinary words to show the whole makes a single code word."

"You know, COBOL seems even easier than BASIC."

"Well, it isn't. Although the instructions are simple enough you must remember that in business there's always this factor

of massive data — a payroll, for example, could involve the wages of 50,000 employees. This means that considerable effort and skill is needed simply organising the data. One approach to this problem, by the way, is to divide the data up into fields, records and files."

"What a mixture — agriculture, hi-fi and ironmongery," mused Fred.

"You could, as an illustration, regard a telephone directory as data so organised," continued Rufus, oblivious to Fred's remark. "A *field* is essentially a basic unit of data for the application involved and so in a telephone directory the name of the person by itself would constitute a field, as would his address and also his telephone number. And a *record* is a collection of inter-related fields. So in our directory the name, address and telephone number of a given person would constitute a record."

"And in the same way a *file* is a collection of records, I suppose — the whole directory, in fact," said Fred in an inspired guess.

"You're absolutely right," confirmed a surprised Rufus. "I expect, then, you'll appreciate only too well that all the files, or directories in an organisation, make up its total data system."

"What else?" replied Fred nonchalantly.

"And I've no need to tell you that many of the address codes used in COBOL — such as PRICE-PER-UNIT — in fact identify fields."

"No need at all."

"Well, I must say you're very well informed," confessed Rufus. "But I do think I'll have to explain that a COBOL program is divided into four parts — or divisions, as they're called. These are the Identification Division, the Environment Division, the Data Division, the Procedure Division — this last being the program proper as you understand the term."

"But what are the three others for, then?" Fred asked.

"Ah, now, it's all very well being able to dream up useful little address names but the computer needs to be told just what names you're going to use and just how much space each field will need in store. And this information is put in the Data Division."

"There are still a couple more."

"They're not very big. The Identification Division in effect merely names the program so that when you pick it up you'll be able to identify it exactly, and the Environment Division details primarily the sort of computer and the peripherals you'll need to run the program and the storage space required."

"Well, perhaps one day you'll teach me how to program in COBOL," said Fred. "But right now I'd like to ask you another question — one I've wanted to ask you almost since we first came into the Language Shop."

"Go ahead," said Rufus.

"What is it that they sell next door?"

For you — specially

"Well, why not go and look for yourself?" suggested Rufus.

Fred hurried through the inter-connecting corridor only to be confronted with a counter bearing a number of strange sounding languages.

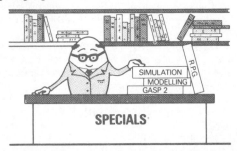

"As you'll recollect," said Rufus who'd followed behind him, "I told you that the general purpose languages we looked at earlier wouldn't be quite as satisfactory as one more specifically tailored to your needs. Here, they try and provide you with just such a tailor-made language."

"You mean, if I really were a chef preparing meals by computer this is the place I'd come to see if there were a language devoted to cookery?"

"Yes, that's the idea."

"But won't each language require its own compiler?"

"It will, and that's something of a drawback, of course."

"Well, there's certainly a lot of languages here. Are there any you'd recommend?"

"There's the Report Program Generator language (RPG) you see there. As you'll appreciate, in business a major form of computer output is the report. The Report Program Generator language enables you to program the computer to produce a report from a given set of files much more easily and quickly than if you used a general purpose language."

At that moment one of the assistants courteously informed them that it was closing time. Fred was rather disappointed.

"Never mind," Rufus consoled him. "You've learnt enough for one day. Why, this morning you didn't even know how pulses controlled the operation of a computer and now you're critically assessing special purpose high-level languages. And don't forget the old saying — 'as one door shuts another opens'."

And looking at his watch Fred saw that Rufus was absolutely right.

5. HOW THE COMPUTER GIVES ORDERS TO ITSELF

"You conceded once," said Rufus the next day, "that computers were very, very fast. Nevertheless, I'm not sure that you appreciate that the CPU is considerably faster than, say the card reader."

"No, not particularly, I'll admit. But does it matter?" asked Fred.

"Well, computer equipment is often very expensive — especially the CPU and the memory. To have such equipment standing idle while, say, the card reader creeps laboriously (relative to the speed of the CPU) through a card reading is nothing but waste. During the time a card is being read the CPU could carry out hundreds of instructions. It's rather as if I asked you to add a column of figures — and then sent you the individual figures at the rate of one a day."

"You mean there'd be plenty of time for me to have a cup of tea? Yes, I see that. But what can you do about it? After all, you have to have the CPU to control the card-reader, don't you?"

"Only for the short time needed to start the operation at the beginning and check at the end that it has been correctly carried out. For the rest of the time it could be used doing other work — such as running a second program."

Multiprogramming

"Are you trying to tell me," asked Fred with a note of disbelief in his voice, "that a computer can handle *two* programs at once?"

"It can handle more than that," replied Rufus. "Provided that it is able to fit all the required programs into its core store at the same time there's no reason theoretically why it can't work on any number at once — or, rather, one at a time but alternating between programs so that when the first program being processed by the CPU reaches a slow card-reading instruction then the CPU is switched to a second program and processes that one until it, in its turn, comes to a slow operation when the CPU is switched back to the first program, or, if that's still not ready, to a third program."

"Guaranteed chaos, if you ask me," muttered Fred. "I can see lots of problems. Data getting read into the wrong program, programs getting mixed up together, the computer forgetting about a program stuck on a card-reader — oh, my goodness, they're endless."

"Well, yes, there have been problems, but these have been solved over the years of computer development. Certainly in the early days of computers it was strictly one program at a time but now it's not only possible but standard practice to have a number of programs all simultaneously in progress, the CPU switching continuously from one to the other as required for the efficient running of the overall operation. This technique is called *multiprogramming.*"

"That's all very well, but you can't just leave a program and come back to it expecting to carry on as if nothing had happened. I mean, think of all the data and half-completed calculations that will have been lost."

"Been lost? What are you talking about? I thought we'd discussed boxes and memory quite enough for you to appreciate that as long as an instruction has been completed all the data will be in boxes — as will the program, of course. So provided you *don't touch that part of the memory where the data and program are stored*, then leaving the program merely freezes everything until the program starts up again. And the results of any half-completed calculations will also be in boxes — they don't float around as pulses."

Control is a steering wheel

"I'm still not clear on just what's happening inside the computer," Fred confessed. "Are all the programs being worked on together?"

"Yes and no," replied Rufus. "Where the peripherals are concerned, yes — where the CPU is concerned, no. In other words, the card-reader can be reading a card relating to one program, the printer can be printing the output of another and the tape-deck recording data for a third — and these operations can all be going on at the same time. But the CPU can *only handle one instruction at a time* so only one program can occupy the CPU's attention at any given moment."

"And the CPU, of course, obeys whatever instruction happens to be in front of it at any given instant?"

"Yes. And we say that the program whose instruction the CPU is obeying has *control*. While that program has control the others can only stand and wait — until, that is, the program reaches a slow operation where control is passed to another program," explained Rufus.

"It sounds as if the CPU has a steering wheel and just one driving-seat — the program in the driving-seat having this control that you are talking about."

"Yes, that's quite a good way to think of it."

"Looking at it through the CPU's eyes, then," said Fred thoughtfully, "all it sees is a single continuous string of instructions — although these will come from different programs."

"That's the idea."

"Right then. But does this mean that a sort of GO TO instruction in one program sends the CPU to an instruction in *another* program because if it does . . . ," and Fred shook his head in wonder as he contemplated the problem.

The operating system — a program with the whip hand

"Yes and no, again," replied Rufus. "Obviously when you're writing a particular program you've no idea which other programs will be running alongside it so it is impossible to insert instructions addressing instructions in other programs — or *pass control*, as we call it. But we can design the computer so that when a program reaches a lengthy peripheral operation control is passed to a permanent 'over-seeing' program and arrange for this to decide which ordinary program should next have control. Such a program is called an *operating system* (or sometimes an executive or control program) and is written with the object of ensuring that the computer processes the ordinary programs as efficiently as possible."

"A program to run a program?" exclaimed Fred. "But if the operating system is itself a program surely it, too, will need the CPU, memory and equipment."

"The CPU and memory, yes, but no equipment — other than the console and some disc storage. However, although the core store must permanently house at least part of the operating system and perhaps devote some 20% of that store to the task, it is still both feasible and economic to accept this memory demand."

"Well, I can certainly see the need for an organising spirit but I can't quite see how a program can fill this need."

"I think," said Rufus thoughtfully, "your difficulty can best be resolved by a discussion with the operating system employed by the University's computer department."

"Discussion with a program? How? A program, you've told me, is no more than a sequence of instructions!"

"Anywhere else in the world I'd agree with you," replied Rufus. "But this is Fredland and anything can happen here."

Fred meets Ossie

In the University computer room the computer operator was just closing down for the day. The whirring and humming of the equipment had died away and when the operator had put out the lights only a dull glow from behind one of the doors in the CPU remained.

"The operating system's in there," whispered Rufus. "His name is Ossie. I'll leave you to sort out your queries with him yourself." And he quietly disappeared.

Fred opened the CPU door and there, looking with interest at a book entitled "Log", sat the operating system looking exactly like what, in fact, he was — an efficient foreman.

"Evenin' sir," Ossie said. "Is there anything I can do for you?"

"Yes," replied Fred. "I'd like to know just how you organise your computer when you're running more than one program at a time."

"Ah, well now, sir, that's quite a biggish task," declared Ossie. "However, with a bit of luck I should be able to give you some idea of how it's done. Now the key to this whole business lies in the fact that I invariably start the day having control and although I always pass this quickly to other programs *it always comes back to me* when a program reaches a point when it cannot immediately use the CPU. That way I keep in charge, as this transfer back to me is automatic."

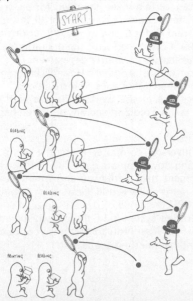

"And how do you decide which program is next to have control?" asked Fred.

How to allocate peripherals and memory

"I think we'd better start at the beginning," Ossie suggested and when Fred nodded his agreement continued, "Now the first thing that happens at the beginning of the day is for me to be given a list of all the programs to be run. Take this morning. As soon as we started They told me They wanted programs Anne, Bess, Claire, Di, Else and Flo to run. Of course, They had also to tell me the priorities of these programs and it so happened they were alphabetically in priority order."

"So after you'd put all the programs into the core store you gave Anne . . . ."

"Steady on, steady on," interrupted Ossie. "We've neither enough equipment nor enough memory to put all that lot on the computer together."

"You haven't?"

"No. I'm afraid our configuration here is limited to 3 tape-decks, 3 VDUs, 2 printers, 1 paper-tape reader, 1 card reader and a 100K memory — together with, of course, a CPU and console."

"What's a 100K memory?" asked Fred.

"Ah, well, you see, we measure memory in thousands of standard-length words — 1,000 such words being symbolised as 'K'."

"So 100K means 100,000 words capacity?"

"That's it. Now, as you'll appreciate, my first job was to ascertain just which and how many of these configuration peripherals each program required, together, of course, with the amount of memory needed. And maybe I should point out that the memory needed was not only to hold the program but also that needed to hold all the data addresses used by the program."

"You say you ascertained all this?"

"Yes. You see, these programs are all on tape with the program requirements listed at the beginning of each program. So all I had to do was extract these details — after which I laid them out, in effect, in a table." Here Ossie proudly showed Fred the morning's table. "As you can see, I've put what we've got available in the last column."

	PROGRAM						AVAILABLE CONFIG.
	A ANNE	B BESS	C CLAIRE	D I	E ELSE	F LO	
PRIORITY	1	2	3	4	5	6	
CARD READERS	1			1			1
PAPER TAPE READERS		1	1				1
MAG. TAPE DECKS		1	1		3	2	3
PRINTERS	1		1	1		1	2
V.D.U'S				1	2	1	3
MEMORY SPACE (Wds K)	25	14	40	17	30	10	80*

* FULL MEMORY SPACE IS 100K BUT 20K IS TAKEN UP BY THE OPERATING SYSTEM LEAVING 80K AVAILABLE

"No, I agree you haven't enough stuff to do all six programs," Fred admitted after studying the table.

"Very well. So my next job is to construct the computer equivalent of a peg-board detailing the computer's configuration and then take the program with the highest priority and allocate to it the facilities it needs on the peg-board."

"You seem to have your memory divided into blocks of 10K," said Fred, looking at Ossie's peg-board.

"Yes. It is, of course, essential for us to keep a careful check on just which memory addresses are being occupied by just what programs. This calls for what is termed a *memory map* that details the memory occupancy — sometimes K by K. But dividing the memory into blocks does give us the simplest method although it often means allocating to a program more memory than the program actually requires — as in the case of Anne here."

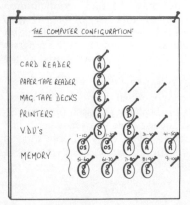

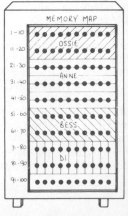

"Fair enough. Well, I see that Anne has also been allocated the card reader and the first printer as well as the three blocks of memory. I suppose, then, you keep taking the programs one by one in priority order and allocating equipment until no more can be squeezed in?"

"That's correct."

"Well, you've easily enough stuff for Bess as well as Anne but there's no second paper-tape reader to cater for Claire, so I suppose Anne and Bess are all you can put on initially."

"And Di," added Ossie. "I know it hasn't as high a priority as Claire but since it only requires facilities that would otherwise lie idle we may as well include it."

"Right. So you've selected Anne, Bess and Di. What now?"

"Now I read all three programs off tape and into core store — storing them, of course, in the part of the memory allocated to them on the memory map."

"Leaving the other three programs on tape," observed Fred. "You know, this creates privileged and unprivileged kinds of programs, doesn't it? I mean, there'll be those privileged programs who are all inside the core store and being processed and those outside on tape impatiently waiting their turn to come in."

"Yes, and of those inside only one at any given moment is actually able to use the CPU."

"So there are two queues, in effect — a queue of programs waiting to go into memory and a queue of those in the memory waiting to go on the CPU."

"You obviously understand the whole process now."

"Not so fast," cried Fred. "I've followed how you queue up

the programs to come into the core store and select the lucky girls to be processed, but I'm not so sure I understand the principle behind the allocation of the *CPU* to programs."

How the programs take turns to steer

"Well," said Ossie, "that's all a matter of passing control. Taking today's run again; once I'd allocated memory and equipment to the three chosen programs I simply had to take the one with the highest priority and hand it control. And this, of course, was Anne. Now it wasn't long before Anne came to a card-reading instruction so once that was started control was returned to me."

"Upon which you handed control to the program with the next highest priority, I suppose," ventured Fred.

"Yes. And after that each time control came to me I simply had to run down the programs in order of priority and hand control to the first of them that happened to be ready to use the CPU. At least, that was all I had to do until one of the programs came to an end."

"I'm still a little unsure as to how you can bounce control backwards and forwards like that — in the context of program instructions, I mean. Could you give me the actual programs together with your own?"

Ossie looked dubious.

"It would mean a rather longish illustration," he replied slowly. "I would rather you just accepted that it could be done. But I'll tell you what," he added seeing Fred's disappointment, "I'll illustrate the technique diagramatically if you like."

And with that Fred had to be satisfied — though he still had one last question on control.

"Look," he said. "It could happen that control was passed to a low priority program which had a considerable amount of cal-

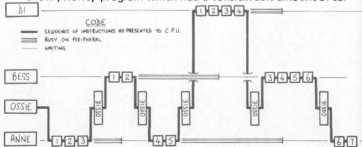

CODE
SEQUENCE OF INSTRUCTIONS AS PRESENTED TO C.P.U.
BUSY ON PERIPHERAL
WAITING

culating to do before it came to a slow operation. Now couldn't that program unfairly hog the CPU for most of the day?"

"Good point," commented Ossie. "But to avoid just that problem every so often — every fifth of a second in the system here — control is *automatically* returned to me. Then I do my usual run down the priorities and see if a program with a higher priority is waiting. Only if one isn't is the interrupted program allowed to continue."

Virtual memory — or how to put a quart into a pint pot

"Tell me," asked Fred, "of all the things that restrict a computer's capacity, which is the most important?"

"Oh, memory, without any question," answered Ossie. "Indeed, the whole size and power of a computer can be measured in terms of memory size."

"So in the case of your computer here which has effectively an 80K memory after allowing for the space you take up yourself it would be quite unable to run a program requiring 160K. So if you wanted to run such a program you'd have to buy another computer."

"My goodness, no." exclaimed Ossie. "That would be a waste since our 80K memory copes adequately with the rest of the work. Buy one with 160K memory and you'll find it will be standing idle for most of the time."

"Well, surely, that's not so intolerable. I mean, I have to have a large dining-table at home so as to be able to seat the whole family when they come to dinner on Sunday. The rest of the week we only use a corner. But what's the alternative?"

"You could have a smaller table and on Sundays eat in sittings — if you're prepared to put up with the inconvenience that is," Ossie pointed out.

"Are you suggesting we should put our programs in the computer memory *in sittings*?" asked an incredulous Fred. "What if a GO TO instruction in one sitting tries to send the computer to an instruction in another sitting. The second instruction won't be there."

"True. But if the programmer knows in advance that his program will be broken down into sittings he can write it so that each sitting is virtually independent of the others. After all, in practice a real program, particularly a long one, tends to have fairly self-contained sections — rather like chapters of a book. Mine, for example, starts with a section dealing with my work from the moment the computer's switched on in the morning until I've identified the first bunch of programs to be 'multi-programmed', then it relates to the second-by-second running of the normal day's work, and finally it deals with the close-down routine. Not much overlapping, really. Of course, on the odd occasions when an unfortunate GO TO cuts across sittings — well, it just means that the current sitting has to be taken out of memory there and then and the new sitting brought in."

"So the programmer has to write his programs in sittings?"

"Yes. Mind you, some sittings will hardly ever sit. When preparing a program you really need to cover every possibility — even the possibility that a person's electricity bill will be F0.00. This means there'll be sections that will only be required if the very rare event transpires. The program, then, will be written so that these sections would only be called into the memory on these rare occasions. This avoids filling up the memory with parts of the program which will never be used in the course of a typical run."

"I accept the principle, but how do you make it work?"

"When the programmer writes his program he will mark the beginning of each such section. Then, when the compiling is

being done the compiler can work out and write at the beginning of the machine coding of each section a statement indicating how much memory space is called for by the section. When that particular section subsequently comes up in the course of the execution of the whole program it is up to me to find an unoccupied part of the memory big enough to hold this section and its associated data. This means, of course, a rather more sophisticated type of memory map than we looked at earlier, but the added complexity is worthwhile."

"What happens if there isn't any room?"

"Then the program has to wait — unless it has a high priority in which case a program in the core store with a low priority is temporarily transferred out of this storage and its place filled by the waiting program."

"There seems to be no end to the tricks a computer can perform," marvelled Fred.

"Possibly not. This particular trick of being able to handle a very large program in a very small memory is referred to as *virtual memory* since the technique in effect provides virtually unlimited memory."

When you come to the end of a perfect program

"You know," said Fred, reflectively, "sooner or later one of these programs must come to an end. What happens then?"

"Nothing complicated, there," replied Ossie. "Once a program's complete it's taken out of core store. With the release of the memory space and facilities I then consider which of the programs still queueing on the tape can be next brought in."

"Using your priority system as a basis of selection and the peg-board to test whether or not a particular program can be fitted in, eh?"

"Yes — just as I did at the beginning. Perhaps I should say that in practice I actually handle priorities in a somewhat more sophisticated manner, but the principle is the same."

"You certainly have plenty to do, don't you?" remarked Fred.

The operating system as a communicator — Ossie the Mouth

"Plenty to do!" echoed Ossie with a hollow laugh. "But that's not the half of it. They want their pound of flesh in this place and that's a fact."

"You've other duties?" blinked Fred.

"You can say that again. To start with I'm expected to tell the operator everything. Just everything."

"I don't quite follow."

"Well, say a program I'm about to start running requires a particular reel of tape (Bess this morning was an example). I have to type on the console all the reel details and the allocated tape deck so the operator can put the right reel on the right deck. Indeed, I have to make sure he's done everything necessary to ensure a smooth program run and if he hasn't then to tell him what's missing. I also have to tell him if anything's gone amiss, such as a card-reader getting jammed."

"Doesn't he ever tell you anything?"

"Well, occasionally. But then it's mostly orders. Run this, alter that — oh, it's a dog's life being an operating system, I can tell you."

"You know, I don't quite see how all this conversation gets done. After all, you're only a program with a very limited vocabulary."

"You certainly know how to hurt, don't you," winced Ossie. "However it's not all that mysterious. All that's necessary is for me to have a complete list of all the instructions the operator is able to give the computer and all the comments I'm allowed to make. These orders and comments can be in plain English or in simple mnemonic or code form."

"But say I was the operator," said Fred "and I typed RUN PROGRAM FLO. What would happen?"

"Well, I'd look down my list of words and find that RUN indicated a new program to be brought on to the computer as soon as possible. I'd then look for PROGRAM FLO on the tape holding the programs and pick up the program requirements listed at the beginning of the program. Then, when the opportunity occurred, I'd put the program on to the computer and type you the message FLO RUNNING. That's unless, of course, the program requires a magnetic tape to be loaded in which case I'd ask you to do that first."

"And what if the thought of Flo running so fascinated me that I forgot to do as you asked?"

"Well, in my case I'm an operating system that's designed to keep reminding you if I find a job's not been done."

"Look after me, do you?"

"All but wet nurse you," growled Ossie.

Other jobs for the operating system

"And what else do you do?" asked Fred.

"Well, computers, you know, are programmed by their manufacturers to double or even treble check all data transfers and calculations. For instance, when data is written on tapes the magnetic coding is immediately read and checked against what should be there — just in case something went wrong during the writing. This ensures an end-product free from error. However, I take note of all such errors requiring correction and if a particular unit starts producing an excessive number of such errors I report the fact to the operator who in turn notifies the engineer that the unit needs attention."

"When I first came in you seemed to be busy with some sort of report or other."

"Yes," Ossie replied. "That was the *log*. It's a record as to how the computer is being used."

"Is that useful, then?"

"Very. If the time that a program begins and ends is recorded you can work out how much computer time it took and so be able to find the cost of running it. Similarly, if each time a magnetic tape is used by a program this is recorded in the log, then if any errors were subsequently found on the tape it would be possible to see which programs may have been using incorrect data. And further analysis of the log will provide you with summaries of how many programs were running at one time and for how long no programs were running — in other words, how long the computer was idle. This sort of information helps plan the work so as to load the computer as evenly as possible."

"Well, well," grinned Fred. "I'm surprised They don't give you a brush to sweep out with while they're at it."

"Shh," hissed Ossie, looking around fearfully. "Don't say things like that."

But the warning came too late, and Ossie is now the only operating system in the world who sweeps the floor.

A discourse on files

On his way out of the University Fred dropped in to say goodbye to Rufus.

"Before you go," said Rufus, "I'd just like to talk to you for a minute or two about files."

"They're not much of a problem, surely," remarked Fred, perching himself on the edge of Rufus's desk. "I remember you defined a file as a collection of records — nothing more, nothing less."

"No, they're no problem as such. As long as the data is put on the (usually) magnetic tape or disc in a logical sequence not much can go wrong. No, it's not so much the technique I'm concerned about as the terminology. For instance, you should be aware that there are basically two kinds of files — one where the data relates to essentially new information (such as goods invoiced to customers during the day) and another kind, called *master files*, where the data relates to relatively unchanging information (such as the address and credit rating of each customer) — though a master file will also often include up-to-date temporary information as well (such as the current indebtedness of each customer). As a matter of fact a customer, or debtors, master file is one of the commonest that there is."

"But surely the current indebtedness would need revising fairly frequently, wouldn't it?"

"Oh yes. Where there is considerable daily trading with a large number of customers then very likely the files of the previous day's sales, sales returns and debtor receipts (each file normally comprising a set of punched cards or length of paper-tape) will be read into the computer together with the customer's master file (this file usually being kept on magnetic tape). The computer will then calculate the new end-of-day indebtedness of each customer and, in addition to printing out any required details of summaries, prepare a new magnetic tape that will incorporate master file data with the new indebtedness. Bringing a master file up-to-date is called *updating*, by the way."

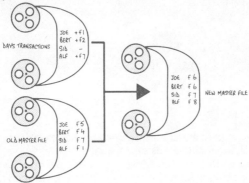

"I've heard people talk of file maintenance. Is that the same thing?"

"No. *File maintenance* is ensuring that the contents of a file are correct. This involves correcting errors (e.g. in the names or addresses of customers), or changing the normally unchanging information (e.g. address or credit ratings) and adding or deleting entries (e.g. when new customers join or old leave)."

"I should imagine it's important not to mix up old and updated tapes or erroneous and corrected tapes," said Fred thoughtfully.

"It's important not to mix up tapes at all," said Rufus tetchily.

"So we need an effective labelling system."

"Yes — one that identifies both the data on the tape and also its date of 'creation'. In addition, chronologically produced tapes are often numbered in sequence — these numbers being called *generation numbers* (where 'generation' is used in the context of forefathers and offspring). Another label detail would be the copy number since on creating any master tape it is sound sense to make at least one copy in case the original becomes lost or damaged.''

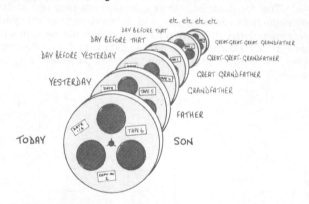

"This means the computer operator has to be very careful when he's writing the labels on the tape."

"It does. But we don't just rely on the operator. Whenever a tape is being created we arrange for the operating system to write the label in magnetic form on the tape itself. And subsequently, before a tape is read, the operating system will first check that the correct tape is in place."

"How will the operating system know if a tape is the correct one or not?"

"My dear Fred, surely by now you are aware that a program on tape or disc contains all the information needed for the operating system to make the cross-check?"

"Poor old Ossie. Always gets the dirty end of the stick."

"You don't want to listen to everything that Ossie says," warned Rufus. "Actually, he's the task-master in the computer room. Always telling the unfortunate operator 'Do this, do that.' Tells him everything he has to do, in fact."

"Does it tell him when he can go for lunch, then?"

"No, not that, I'll admit," replied Rufus. "They have another device for that. It's called a CLOCK."

Error Detection and Correction

Computers handle data rapidly and invisibly. It is, therefore, impossible to check errors manually, so every time the computer carries out any operation, be it the execution of a program instruction, fetching information from its memory, or passing data to or from a reading, storage, or printing device it has to check *for itself* that the operation was carried out correctly.

Error detection, then, is a major function of a computer in addition to its normal processing work. The methods of error detection — and their frequently associated techniques of *error correction* — depend upon the potential location and nature of such errors and are far too various to be detailed here. One common form of error can, however, be briefly mentioned. This relates to detecting *bit errors*.

As we've seen, bits are pulses and magnetic spots. Now stray pulses in the system arising from specks of dust on magnetic surfaces can result in a byte either acquiring or losing a bit at some stage. To detect such a gain or loss the circuitry is designed to add a '1' or a '0' to the end of every byte — the addition being such that the byte in total contains *an even number of '1's* (or, in an alternative system, an odd number of '1's). This additional bit is called a *parity bit*. Each time a byte is read or moved a test is made to see if there are an even number of '1's. If there are not, the system signals an error.

Now, surprising as it may seem, it is possible for the computer itself to correct an erroneous byte, though the error correction technique does call for a further set of parity bits. The principle is to 'lay out' the bytes (with the parity bits) in vertical blocks, each block then being given a further byte (a *parity byte*) constructed so that each bit *column* again has an even number of '1's. In such circumstances a bit error will result in error detection being signalled in both the byte and the column — and where byte and column intersect, there lies the error. Correction then involves no more than a reversal of the offending bit. [Continued overleaf

Be an error correction routine

Detect the error in the left-hand block and detect and correct the error in the right-hand block:

BYTE NUMBER	PARITY BIT ↓		PARITY BIT ↓
1	01001111 1		01100101 0
2	01010100 1		00100011 1
3	01100000 0		01000101 0
4	00000010 1		01110101 1
5	00101111 0		00000100 1
6	01110000 1		01101010 0
7	00011010 1		00011101 0
		PARITY BYTE ➤	00010101 1

ANSWER

Left-hand block: error in byte number 5.
Right-hand block: error in byte number 3, 4th bit. Should be 010101010.

Note that this error correction technique can even lead to the correction of an erroneous parity bit (or parity byte), for if a parity bit (byte) were wrong then the technique would signal a wrong parity column (byte) as well as a normal row (column). Correction would involve bit reversal at the intersection as usual.

6. THE MATING GAME
or, choosing the computer in your life

"My boss," groaned Fred in a hollow voice the following week, "says we're going to be computerised."

"Well, why so gloomy?" asked Rufus. "For the past six months you've been complaining bitterly that it just wasn't possible for your office to cope with the paper-work. Indeed, if I remember rightly, you said the May report didn't go out until September. Now perhaps your reports will be out by the first of the following month."

"Oh, yes, there's no doubt *that* will be speeded up. I'm not sure though, that the object of the exercise isn't to enable our Chairman to impress his colleagues in other companies — though I suppose if he wants to spend the company's money in that way it won't actually *harm* the office efficiency."

"As a matter of fact it could," said Rufus. "Though it's unlikely. But I would certainly never advocate computerisation for its own sake. It's not only wasteful of time and money but the end result may well be a less flexible system. You must remember that once you get a computer then, if it's to be used at all efficiently, jobs have to be fairly rigorously scheduled. And this means in turn that you can't do them as and when you feel like it but only as and when the schedule says. It also means that making changes becomes much more complicated and expensive."

"You mean you're very much tied down?"

89

"Yes. Mind you. being tougher on scheduling and procedures is not necessarily a bad thing since it tightens up work
discipline throughout the office. But loss of flexibility must
always be borne in mind when deciding whether or not to
computerise. However, you haven't answered my question —
why so gloomy?"

"Because I've been given the job," replied Fred sadly, "of
selecting the computer."

Thou shalt not be wise after the event

"I'd have thought a man of your talents would have had
little difficulty handling that," said Rufus.

"Well, I'd feel happier," replied Fred, "if I could be sure of
getting a reliable answer from those computer people. I've
noticed such folk have a marked tendency to say 'Oh, that's
no problem' if you ask them about the possibility of a particular
job being done, but when it comes to the crunch it's 'Well,
it's not so easy as that', or, 'Yes, but you'll need a lot more
equipment to do it properly' — and so on."

"Yes, I know what you mean. But there are good reasons
behind this, you know. It arises in any situation where there
are pre- and post-equipment periods. Say you were to tell a
lift manufacturer that you wanted a lift that would take eight
people up to the sixth floor in one minute. He may well say
'No problem' and install such a lift for you. But if you then
said you wanted it to stop at the intermediate floors as well he
could possibly reply in the way your computer people do.
After all, the lift wasn't designed to do that."

"But any fool knows a lift needs to stop at all floors,"
growled Fred.

"Some lifts don't you know. But I chose the obvious
example to make my point. The thing is, a computer installation can be designed to give you virtually anything you specify
in advance, but it cannot necessarily be adapted to give you
what you want *after* installation."

"You mean that you can't just go out and buy a computer?
That you need to know just what you want your computer to
do *before* you start?"

"Most certainly I do. And, just as important, what you will
want your computer to do in the more distant future. Otherwise you're pretty certain to end up with the wrong one. Don't

forget the term 'computerisation' covers a spectrum running from small ledger accounting machines at one end to large, multi-terminal systems at the other. So you must start by making a *systems survey* which will indicate *exactly* what your requirements are and how they're currently being met."

Fred's system surveyed . . .

"And how precisely do you go about that?" asked Fred.

"Well, essentially it's a matter of deciding *who* needs *what*, and *when* and *how* it's to be provided," replied Rufus. "Fred,

correct me if I'm wrong but don't you and Freda run a boarding kennels on the side?"

"Well, yes. But Freda does most of the work. I just do an odd hour or two a day — sort of managing really."

"Then let's assume you're to get a computer to help you."

"But the size of my turnover would never justify the cost of a computer," gasped Fred.

"No, but it will serve as an illustration. Now, who needs data in your kennel business?"

"Well, I do, and so does Freda. Oh, and we've a part-time accountant who needs some, too."

"Good. So our systems survey has identified the 'who'. Next, what information do the three of you need?"

"For myself, since I handle the bookings, I need to know the current bookings and also the future unbooked capacity so that I can see if I can accept an offered booking. I need to know, too, how the takings are going and also if any dogs booked for the previous day haven't arrived. Finally, I need to have details of all our clients. As for Freda, she needs to know which dogs are arriving and which are leaving the next day and to have a report showing just where every dog is kennelled. Oh, and she'd find a list of empty kennels useful, too."

"And the accountant?"

"He only needs to know the day after a dog leaves how many days it was boarded and the daily rate — and, periodically, the debtors position. And he, too, needs to have details of all our clients."

"So that's the 'what'. Next, the 'when'."

"Daily, of course (apart from the debtors). We like to keep our fingers on the pulse, you know."

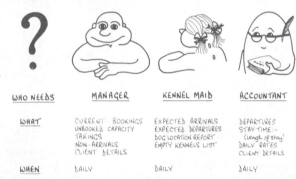

WHO NEEDS	MANAGER	KENNEL MAID	ACCOUNTANT
WHAT	CURRENT BOOKINGS UNBOOKED CAPACITY TAKINGS NON-ARRIVALS CLIENT DETAILS	EXPECTED ARRIVALS EXPECTED DEPARTURES DOG LOCATION REPORT EMPTY KENNELS LIST	DEPARTURES STAY TIME:— (length of stay) DAILY RATES CLIENT DETAILS
WHEN	DAILY	DAILY	DAILY

"As a matter of interest, how is this information currently recorded and distributed?" asked Rufus.

"Well," replied Fred vaguely, "at the moment we just have the stuff around in the office and everybody hunts for what they want."

"Thus conforming to the principle of keeping one's finger on the pulse, I suppose," remarked Rufus drily. "Well, I think we can improve on that. Incidentally, when making a systems survey you'll often find quite large anomalies in the existing system — both in respect of information produced and also in the way it's being produced. In your case I suspect that both you and the accountant each have your own list of clients that are to all intents and purposes identical."

"How did you know that," exclaimed Fred. "Why, I only found out myself last week."

"Since the survey's shown you both need that information then under the crude system you have it's probable you'll each obtain it independently."

"Crude system it might be," muttered Fred under his breath, "but I bet my kennels make more money than your books."

... and Fred's system designed

"Having done the survey," continued Rufus, oblivious of Fred's comment, "we can turn to the *systems design* which re-designs the whole system in general terms. Such a design eliminates all the anomalies thrown up by the survey (such as your duplicated clients' list) and of itself goes a long way to improving the efficiency of the overall system."

"And what will the systems design for my kennels look like?" asked Fred.

"Well, on the information you gave me I'd say that to start with you need a Booking form — no, better a Booking/Cancellation form — looking like this," replied Rufus sketching rapidly. "From this your computer will be able to produce your Bookings schedule and your Unbooked Capacity report as well as Freda's Expected Arrivals report. Now in addition I think you ought to have a Registration form like this," and Rufus added a second sketch to the first, "from which you can produce your Dog Location report (which will include your list of empty kennels) and your Tomorrow's Departures report."

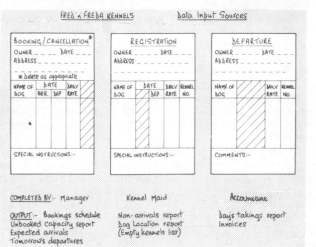

"And, I suppose, we'll need a Departure form as well?"

"Yes — and that together with the Registration form will enable you to produce a Day's Takings report and your accountant to prepare the clients' invoices," said Rufus sketching the last of the forms. "You'll notice, by the way, that with appropriately placed carbons completing the first form results in most of the other two being completed at the same time."

"Well, that's certainly a lot better," admitted Fred.

"More to the point, said Rufus, "you've now some idea just what your computer has to do."

Pieces of input

"Which will help me decide on the computer I need," remarked Fred. "I suppose to a large extent that will depend on how long and complicated the programs are."

"Well, not particularly," replied Rufus. "Though I'll admit that the length and complexity of the programs do have some bearing on the matter. However, much more significant is the actual number of *pieces of data input* that must be processed in a given time. Don't forget that the CPU can handle hundreds of instructions — as opposed to pieces of input — in a very, very brief period. It's the volume of data that needs to be read, transferred and handled generally that takes the time and determines the basic computer configuration."

"And what exactly is a 'piece of input data'?" asked Fred.

"Well, take your kennel business. How many bookings and cancellations do you have per day?"

"Taken together, about 20."

"And registrations?"

"It averages around 15."

"So there must be some 15 departures a day as well. In total, then, you'll have 20 + 15 + 15 = 50 pieces of input data a day — quite apart from any other work you might put on the computer."

"And where do I go from there?"

"Well, you then decide how long each piece of input will take to process and how much output each piece will generate. Knowing this it's possible to calculate the hardware units required and also the number of master files needed."

"Master files? What master files do I need in the kennel business?"

"There's your clients' list, to start with — though that will only require file maintenance. For daily updating you'll need a Bookings file and Dog Location file. I'm assuming, by the way, that for simplicity of illustration your accountant will use a manual debtors accounting system."

"How the deuce does all this fit together?" asked Fred.

"We'll discuss that when we come to systems analysis," Rufus promised. "Let me just remind you of your output which, in addition to some 15 invoices a day, will include daily reports on current bookings, future unbooked capacity, expected arrivals, dog location, expected departures and takings."

"Some output," whistled Fred. "And it's all got to be printed. I seem to remember you saying that printing was relatively slow, so won't the volume of printing come into the calculations?"

"It certainly will. Printing is in practice a notorious bottleneck since a little processing can at times create hours of printing. For instance, on an average computer, the program 1 . . . FOR N = 1 to 1000 2 . . . PRINT N*N 3 . . . NEXT N 4 . . . END would take under 5 seconds to process but a minute or more to print."

Think how you input

"Another thing you have to consider," continued Rufus, "is the method of input."

"I thought all input was in the form of punched cards or tape," said Fred.

"That certainly was the case, and it was once just a matter of deciding if the input data was to be in the form of records of much the same size — in which case punched cards were called for — or in the form of records of varying length and content, when punched paper tape was the answer. However, times are changing and the cheaper electronic components now available have led to devices which enable you to code direct on to magnetic tape, and even magnetic disc."

Rufus then went on to explain that for other types of encoding special input devices were needed on the main computer system. These devices usually related to special applications such as magnetic ink character recognition for bank cheques (MICR), optical character recognition readers for documents (OCR) and mark-sensing devices that "read" pencil marks made in certain areas of specially printed documents.

How much computer?

"By the time you've reached this point," continued Rufus (I'll be a nervous wreck, Fred muttered to himself), "you should be able to decide when jobs will run and the time they will take. This will enable you to draw up a *computer usage chart* from which you will be able to identify peak load conditions. Don't forget, by the way, that almost certainly input data will occasionally be delayed causing the actual peaks to be somewhat higher than those shown by a study assuming perfect scheduling."

"As if I would," said Fred ironically. "Tell me, Rufus — just what would this computer usage chart look like?"

"Well in the case of your kennels it could look something like this," replied Rufus sketching quickly.

COMPUTER USAGE CHART — INPUTS

	MON	TUE	WED	THUR	FRI	SAT	SUN
BOOKINGS	20	30	35	35	35	50	40
DOG LOCATION	20	10	20	30	30	60	40
TAKINGS	20	10	20	30	30	60	40
OTHER (Estimated)	30	30	10	10	10	–	–
TOTAL THEORETICAL USAGE	90	80	85	105	105	170	120
ASSUME 20 INPUT CARRY-OVER FROM PREVIOUS DAY	20	20	20	20	20	20	20
PROBABLE ACTUAL USAGE	110	100	105	125	125	190	140

∴ COMPUTER TO BE ABLE TO COPE WITH 190 INPUT UNITS IN A SINGLE DAY

"And that would give me a good lead as to the computer I'd need?"

"It's one of the more important factors, certainly," Rufus agreed.

To have and to hold

"There are, however," Rufus went on, "a couple of other points that should be considered which large-scale users at present seem to fail to appreciate fully. The first of these is the risk an organisation may run of very serious trouble should there be any prolonged interruption in the computer processing caused by outside factors."

"Are you suggesting," asked Fred in surprise, "that organisations can become so dependent on their computer systems that they cannot be without them for more than a few hours?"

"Well, they'll get by but their efficiency may be drastically reduced in such circumstances. This is particularly so when they rely more and more on information from their computer systems to make day-to-day decisions. Trying to make decisions in such circumstances without up-to-date information can lead to highly expensive and embarrassing errors. If you've failed to get your Future Occupancy report, for instance, you could unwittingly accept bookings when there were no free kennels, or conversely turn away profitable bookings when there were."

"I see. And what's the other thing that tends to be over-looked?"

"The problem of physical security," replied Rufus. "Of course, the most widely adopted precaution is storing magnetic tape in a fire-proof safe, but even better is keeping copies in a separate location. In addition the hardware also needs protection, and there's the problem of guarding against unauthorised access to the software or the hardware. To handle this, automatic locks have been designed that can be opened only by magnetic cards or keys — such locks providing you with a complete list at the end of the day of the cards used to open them."

"So one has to consider all these non-computing points when deciding just what is required in the way of a computer system?"

"I'm afraid so," apologised Rufus.

How big?

"What choice is there of computers?" asked Fred. "I mean, how big and small are the computers available to us?"

"Well," replied Rufus, "if we exclude the visible record computers that are available, a small computer might typically consist of a central processing unit with 20 − 40,000 bytes of main memory, a punched card reader/sorter, a line printer, some disc storage (say 10 million bytes) and a console. The peripheral units are, of course, connected to the CPU by direct cabling and these cables are known as *channels* — the number of which are given as part of the specification of a configuration."

"One reader/sorter, one printer, one disc unit, one console — I make that four units," observed Fred, counting on his fingers the peripherals named.

"So that means it's a four-channel system."

"And how sophisticated would a system like that be?"

"Generally speaking, it could run one program at a time and simulataneously transfer data from a punched card on to disc or transfer data for printing from disc to the printer."

"If you were to start with a small computer like that could you enlarge it later if you wanted?"

"Oh, yes. Usually the next step up from such a configuration would be the addition of more memory, more disc capacity and the inclusion of magnetic tape units — together, of course, with the necessary channels. Simple multi-programming could then be used if desired."

"And if you wanted an even bigger computer you could just add more units, I suppose."

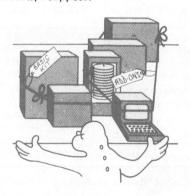

"Well, there are usually upper limitations on configurations for various models — there may just not be enough physical capacity to add more channels or memory in certain cabinets

or the CPU may not be fast enough to handle the extra work. So it is important to select a computer that will allow you to add to its initial load as much work as you're likely to want it to do over the future years."

"It seems, then, that choosing a computer is more a matter of what you will want in the future than what you will want now," observed Fred.

"I think that's a fair statement," said Rufus. "It is, of course, extremely difficult to predict the future but any organisation requiring a computer should normally make some projection of future needs. It should also try to define the logical moments at which the configuration might be expanded and new work taken on so that the final configuration can be arrived at without any traumatic changes having to take place along the way. This is important since there would almost certainly be a serious disruption of current work if a major change were ever required. The problem of forecasting is unfortunately made considerably harder by the rate of technological progress. New systems and devices are launched on to the market so rapidly that applications that were once impossible become feasible overnight."

"I suppose that in the main you should look to the largest sized computer you're ever likely to need and base your initial configuration, as you call it, on that," hazarded Fred.

"Not necessarily," replied Rufus. "It's not always true of a computer system to say that bigger is better. Being able to add a second processor to a system instead of doubling the speed of the one already installed or, indeed, installing a second computer system linked to the existing one rather than adding large amounts of new equipment, can equally well provide the required capacity and, at the same time, also offer security in the event of equipment failure."

"You mean that instead of having a possible total stoppage

of work half the system at least can be kept going? Yes, that's a good point."

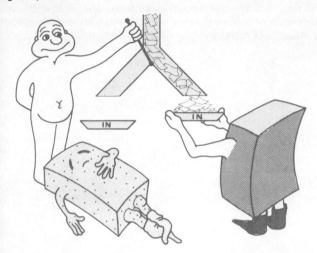

Into the market place

"Once you've done all this," continued Rufus, "you should have a good idea as to the computer configuration you will want. So the next step is to see exactly what's on offer. This involves obtaining detailed quotes of configurations and costs from various manufacturers."

"Well, yes, that's obvious," said Fred. "But how does one choose between the different configurations offered?"

"I'm afraid you've little option but to rely very much on the manufacturers' specialists," Rufus admitted. "And since similar claims will probably come from competing manufacturers the choice can prove difficult. In such circumstances you may well need to place emphasis on the reputation of a particular manufacturer. Don't forget, too, that any support facilities offered have to be taken into account."

"Sounds rather like when you buy your first car," Fred observed ruefully. "Everybody but you knows just what is involved."

"You're right," agreed Rufus. "The problem is very similar and the final choice between makes and models can, in practice, often hinge on the little things. However, for a really big computer system you can often insist upon a series of test and demonstrations being undertaken. The particular combination of tests you select is known as a *benchmark* because the performance of a given system whilst running these tests provides a measure of its power vis-a-vis a rival system.''

"What sort of costs are we talking about when we think in terms of a computer system?'' asked Fred.

"An impossible question to answer,'' replied Rufus. "The range is enormous, and the systems available so varied that i is difficult to be specific. Not only that, but prices change al the time. Moreover, for a medium to large installation it i usual to have a purpose-built computer room with air-condition ing and this represents another expensive item. Add to that th cost of the manufacturer's maintenance contract and it become obvious that a computer installations calls for a lot of carefu thought.''

"I think one of our problems will be finding the capital to buy the monster,'' said Fred.

"Oh, but you don't necessarily have to buy it outright i you don't want. You can often either rent it on a monthly basis or lease it from a leasing company. But this is really matter that should be left to your accountant. You may though, be interested to know that there have been move of late by customers away from purchase (or leasing) to renting — partly because less capital is tied up and partly because the rate of technological change is now such that there may be advantages in being able to trade-in certain units for the latest models as they appear."

Yea or nay

"I should think," said Fred thoughtfully, "that if you weren't careful you could easily end up with a computer that was, in fact, quite uneconomic."

"Very easily," agreed Rufus. "One of the simplest ways of losing large sums of money is indeed to buy a configuration that is totally unsuitable for the work it will have to deal with. Your kennels, for instance, do not warrant a computer — an intelligent paper routine using multiple copies of your forms would be quite adequate."

"That's an obvious case. But what do you do in less obvious cases?"

"Well, it's really a matter of bringing together the computer running costs (which will be indicated by your systems design and usage chart), and savings that will follow the abandonment of the existing system, the value of the additional information that will be produced (and that includes the value of convenience and speed), and the amount of money available for buying the computer. Making, in fact, what is sometimes called a *feasibility study* — often a major operation."

"What would you do if using a computer would give you worthwhile savings on a few short-run jobs but such savings would never cover the cost of a full computer set-up?"

"Then you can use the services of a computer bureau," Rufus replied. "But we'll talk about that another day."

"Suits me," agreed Fred. "It looks as if you've already loaded me with a systems survey, a systems design, a pieces-of-input count, a data input decision, a computer-usage charting, a security problem, a long-term computer configuration forecast and a financial analysis. Quite enough for me to be going on with until the day after tomorrow."

"My dear Fred," exclaimed a startled Rufus, "you'll never do all that in a day!"

" 'Course I won't," grinned Fred. "But that's all the time it will take me to set up a sub-committee and delegate the work to it. Oh, and I'm going to arrange for the Company to have you seconded — and appointed committee chairman."

And Fred did just that.

7.
THE HUMAN SIDE OF COMPUTING

"I studied your report," said Fred sourly some weeks later, "and then put to the Board a recommendation which was accepted."

"Then why are you so upset?" asked Rufus.

"Because they considered that I'd done such a good job that they appointed me the Data Processing Manager."

"I fear, Fred, that you have an innate distaste for responsibility. I'm sure you were happiest when you were selling ice-cream in Cee. Never mind. You've succeeded in convincing them you know how to select a computer — now let's see you convince them that you are a superlative Data Processing Manager."

"You mean you'll stay on my committee?" Fred asked hopefully.

"I never said that," Rufus replied sharply. "But I'll help you get started. First, do you know what the job entails?"

In the beginning there's a need

"I suppose it means getting the computer to churn out its stuff," Fred hazarded.

"It means much more than that," Rufus said. "It also means providing a specialist service to managers, telling them just what the computer can give them and just what they have to give the computer to get it. You know, managers often appreciate what information would be of value to them but knowing how that information can be extracted from the data that flows through their departments is quite another matter. This is the domain of specialist staff from your department who must, then, liaise closely with these managers so that a system can be devised that ultimately provides the required information."

"So I'll start by asking the managers what it is they want."

"It's not quite that easy," cautioned Rufus. "Managers often find it difficult to state unambiguously to an 'outsider' just what they do want. The Data Processing Manager may well find himself in the position of the man who, after hearing an inspiring speech on how the lot of the human race could be improved by the efforts of individuals, asked what he could do to help and received the reply, 'Even more.' "

"All right — instead of asking them I'll cross-examine them to find out exactly what it is they want."

"You should check, too, that such information is economically worthwhile. Some information is just not worth the cost of its production — though managers cannot be expected to know this since they won't know what its provision will entail. Conversely, as Data Processing Manager you won't know the value of the information to the manager."

"Yes, I see it's more than a matter of just asking them," admitted Fred — an admission he made even more fully when Rufus pointed out that the *frequency* of reporting information was also a matter of joint consideration since the greater the frequency the greater the value to the manager but the greater the cost of preparation.

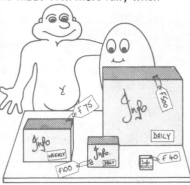

Who's who in Data Processing

"I'll have to have staff," said Fred. "I can't do all that *and* look after the processing."

"You'll certainly need staff," agreed Rufus. "And because the over-all work of the department divides logically into designing the systems, writing the programs and operating the computer we usually have systems analysts, programmers and computer operators to handle each aspect of the work."

"Sort of specialists in a specialist department."

"That's right. The *systems analyst* has the job of providing the link between the department and the rest of the organisation — or, if you like, of reconciling the manager's dreams with the computer's capability. To do this he designs a practical data-handling system that best meets the manager's require-

ments in the most economical manner. This he describes in considerable detail. From the systems analyst's design the *programmer* writes the complete programs. Finally the *computer operator* actually operates the computer and the computer, hopefully, produces the required information."

"That's my full staff?"

"In the main, yes, though there are one or two support groups such as card punchers, librarians and data control (people responsible for seeing the data goes into the system and is processed completely) who also help," Rufus replied.

Get it down

"It seems a long way from start to finish," sighed Fred "Still, let's get going and see just what these people have to do so that the department is a loved rather than unloved child.'

"Well, there's one important point I'd like to get across to you right from the start," said Rufus. "You know, it's rarely appreciated by the layman (and occasionally even overlooked by computer personnel) that *documentation* is absolutely critical. It's no use just evolving a system as you go and leaving it at that. Everything that a computer and the user department has to do and the exact way it must be done must be written down in the form of a permanent record."

"Why?" asked Fred. "Personally I'm a great believer in the flexible, *laissez-faire*, cross-one's-bridges-when-one-comes-to-them method of working."

"And in computer systems that method has absolutely nothing to commend it. To start with, Fred, the whole data-processing machinery is so highly integrated — with the simple-minded computer at the centre of the whole system — that your flexible human clerk can create havoc by inserting data in what appears to be a common-sense manner. If, for example, he wrote an infant's age in years on a form anticipating months the computer would signal a child prodigy. So it is important that people both know, and have a record of, exactly what they are to do. Moreover, if people can also look up what their colleagues are to do they can intelligently respond to unusual circumstances and record data in a manner that will be sensibly incorporated into the final output rather than stimulate nonsense."

"All right — point taken," conceded Fred.

"Oh, but there's more to it than just that. Good documentation enables the user to see precisely what he can get out of the system and so utilise its maximum potential rather than put up with a less-than-adequate service. And don't forget, either, that people leave, and without documentation their successors will take a long time mastering the job thoroughly — if at all."

"I should imagine there's quite a bit of documentation, then."

"There certainly is. In the main it comprises systems definitions, clerical manuals, program specifications and operating instructions. And we'll look at each of these in turn later."

What the systems analyst does

"Well, can we start now?" asked Fred.

"Yes," replied Rufus. "And first we'll look at what the systems analyst does."

Rufus then went on to explain that the systems analyst had the task of:

✳ Determining the correctness of a statement by distinguishing between fact, surmise and opinion.

✳ Detailing how data is to be treated so that it arrives in the Data Processing Department ready for punching.

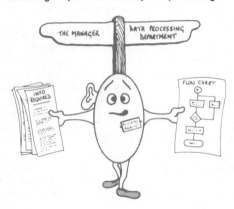

✳ Detailing how the system is to be divided up into individual programs.

✳ Integrating all procedures in the user departments so that the system is free from all potential hold-ups.

✳ Preparing flow charts that detail the data flow and checking these charts to ensure that the relevant data is collected and treated in the most efficient and effective manner possible.

✳ Ensuring that the user understands just what he'll get out of the system and that it may not be possible in future to add something omitted at the systems design stage.

"Like getting a lift to stop at all floors," remembered Fred.

"Just so," said Rufus. "And he also has to ensure that every possible piece of data is catered for, however freakish (such as a debtor owing zero Fredsticks), otherwise there'll be trouble."

"Sounds like hard work to me."

"It is. And in one respect the harder the better for it pays to take considerable pains in this work otherwise you can devise and all but implement a system and then discover from, perhaps, a casual conversation that there exists some factor which makes all your efforts a waste of time."

"Rather like a man who agrees to paint the outside of his friend's house while his friend is on holiday and while chatting to the milkman as he is finishing learns that his friend's house is the one opposite?"

"That sort of thing, yes."

"You know," said Fred, "this word 'system'. It seems to be used very glibly. Can you give me an example of a system?"

"Well, it has been defined as a set of integrated procedures. Take your kennel business, for example. We have, in fact, already done part of the systems analyst's work by preparing that brief systems design — the most detailed part of which was the forms design."

"Yes, and you talked about one or two master files and promised me you'd show me how it all fitted together."

"Detail the system, in fact. Well, what about this?" asked Rufus producing a sheaf of papers. "The input, you'll remem-

FRED 'n' FREDA KENNELS: REPORT OUTPUTS —

BOOKINGS SCHEDULE   DATE

OWNER	DOG	DATES			DAILY RATE
		BOOKING	ARRIVAL	DEPART	

UNBOOKED CAPACITY   DATE

DATE	KENNELS	
	BOOKED	FREE

TOMORROW'S DEPARTURES   DATE

| OWNER | DOG | KENNEL No |
| | | |

NON-ARRIVALS   DATE

| OWNER | DOG | DATE of BOOKING | COMMENTS * |
| | | | |

* Inserted manually

DOG LOCATION   EVENING OF:

OWNER	DOG	KENNEL No	DATES	
			ARRIVAL	DEPARTURE

EMPTY KENNELS LIST:

EXPECTED ARRIVALS   DATE

| OWNER | DOG | EXPECTED DEP. DATE | KENNEL No * |
| | | | |

* Inserted manually by Kennel Maid

DAYS TAKINGS   DATE

OWNER	DOG	DATES		No. DAYS	DAILY RATE	INVOICE AMOUNT
		ARR.	DEP.			

DAYS TOTAL
OLD YEAR-TO-DATE
NEW YEAR-TO-DATE

ber, comes from the three forms we discussed when we talked about systems designs. Our report outputs are the reports shown here (together with the daily invoices) which we briefly mentioned at the same time.''

"All very pretty, but I still don't see how they fit together," said Fred after studying the reports closely.

"Of course you don't," snapped Rufus. "I haven't shown you yet. Now first I must tell you that under this system it is necessary to punch a card for every dog and that for identification purposes the owner's name followed by the dog's name forms a composite name that I'll refer to as NAME. If you recollect I said that the Bookings and Location master files were updated daily. I think you'll see from this table how it all fits." And Rufus pointed to a paper head INPUT/OUTPUT TABLE.

FRED 'N' FREDA KENNELS: INPUT/OUTPUT TABLE

(Note: MF = Master file)

ROUTINE	INPUT	MASTER FILE RECORD	OUTPUT
BOOKINGS	Old BOOKINGS MF Day's BOOKINGS/ CANCELLATIONS Day's REGISTRATIONS	NAME, date of booking, booked arrival date, booked departure date, daily rate.	New BOOKINGS MF BOOKINGS SCHEDULE NON-ARRIVALS report EXPECTED ARRIVALS report UNBOOKED CAPACITY report
DOG LOCATION	Old LOCATION MF Day's REGISTRATIONS Day's DEPARTURES	NAME, arrival date, booked departure date, kennel no.	New LOCATION MF DOG LOCATION report TOMORROW'S DEPARTURES report
TAKINGS	Old TAKINGS MF Day's REGISTRATIONS Day's DEPARTURES	NAME, arrival date, daily rate. (Total takings for year to date at very end of file)	New TAKINGS MF DAY'S TAKINGS report INVOICE file
INVOICING	CLIENTS MF INVOICE tape	Owner's name, address, telephone no., credit terms, address to which invoice should be sent. MISC	Daily INVOICES INVOICE TOTAL/ DAY'S TAKINGS reconciliation.

"You've seen what's on the forms," Rufus continued as Fred took the paper, "and I've indicated what is in each master file record so you can see that by bringing together all the input and master file data it's possible to produce each output stated."

"Does this mean," said Fred, looking at the outputs unbelievingly, "that when you update a master file you re-write the whole file every day?"

"Oh, yes. For a computer, re-writing the entire file while incorporating the new data is a trivial operation. Moreover in practice the DOG LOCATION and TAKINGS routine would be probably carried out as a single operation (with the INVOICING routine thrown in, too, maybe). However, treating them separately like this does help simplify the system and make it easier to explain."

"Simplify it it might," remarked Fred, "but I still wouldn't know how to make it work."

The systems definition

"Well, I haven't finished yet," replied Rufus petulantly. "Don't keep trying to run before you can walk. Now having designed the system the analyst then has to prepare a *systems definition*. This documents the whole system and falls into two parts — one part stating accurately and unambiguously exactly what the system is required to do and also what information goes in and comes out and in what format. It also details in full all the necessary clerical procedures.

"And the other part?"

"That details the program specifications from which the programmer writes the programs — and its preparation is often delegated to a senior programmer. But we'll look at that later. I should tell you that the first part includes preparing sample reports so that the user can see and approve the sort of information the system will be giving him. Indeed, it is important to keep the user fully involved in all respects as the definition work progresses and equally important to make sure that right from the outset the user staff realise how much time they will be required to give to the project. There is nothing worse for an analyst than trying to get facts from people who are too busy to give them. User staff will also be required to find time to review the final system and — most important — to signify their agreement to it before any programming work starts. This makes the user responsible for the final check that the facts are right."

Rufus then went on to explain that it was also important at this stage for the analyst to outline to the user any changes in the current method of working which would be advantageous to the smooth running of the computer system. This enables plans to be drawn up to help the ultimate change to the new method of working to take place in an orderly way rather than as a great rush at the last minute.

The clerical procedures

"Going back to this kennels business of mine," said Fred. "I'd very much like to look at the clerical procedures you feel are necessary."

"Ah, yes," nodded Rufus. "The clerical procedures are without doubt very important since what comes out of a computer is completely dependent upon what goes in. More specifically, the quality and accuracy of input determines the usefulness of the output."

"You mean if you put false data in you'll get misleading output."

"Precisely. Computer people refer to this as **GIGO** — if you put **G**arbage **I**n you'll get **G**arbage **O**ut. Don't forget that a computer cannot reason for itself and if by accident you write that you can average 8150 km per hour in your car instead of 81.50, then the computer will solemnly assure you that you could drive round the world in under five hours."

"So when you hear about computers making silly mistakes, it's not really their fault at all?"

"No. Only rarely is it the computer's fault. Almost invariably they arise, in fact, from badly specified systems (as in the legendary demand for F0.00) or poorly controlled input (as in our round-the-world car speed example)."

"Obviously low-quality personnel," sniffed Fred. "That won't happen in my department."

"Not always a matter of quality. Often one just fails to appreciate how computers will react to unusual input. One computer, for instance, engaged on translation from English into another country's language, rendered the saying 'out of sight, out of mind' as 'invisible idiot'."

"But my kennels . . . " said Fred drawing Rufus back to his earlier request.

"Oh, I've got the outline clerical procedures for those here," replied Rufus pulling out another sheet of paper. "Written out in full detail they would, of course, be much longer."

While Fred studied Rufus's sheet Rufus went on to explain that a very important part of the systems definition was the *clerical manual*. In a more complex business than Fred's kennels such a manual would describe the routines to be followed in the preparation, batching, input and filing of the input documents. The manual, which would be built up as the system developed, would, among other things, explain the proper way to fill in each document, the original source of the information entered on the document, and the effect such information would have on the files in the system.

FRED 'n' FREDA KENNELS: CLERICAL MANUAL detailing
CLERICAL PROCEDURES

On receipt of a booking or cancellation:

Kennel manager to:

1. Complete BOOKING/CANCELLATION multiple form.
2. Delete either 'BOOKING' or 'CANCELLATION'.
3. If part cancellation received cancel _entire_ booking (as shown in BOOKING SCHEDULE) and re-book.
4. Pass BOOKING/CANCELLATION copy to Data Processing Department
5. Pass REGISTRATION and DEPARTURE copies (attached) to Kennel Maid.

On arrival of dog(s):

Kennel Maid to:

1. Complete REGISTRATION double form.
2. Select appropriate kennel from EMPTY KENNELS LIST at bottom of DOG LOCATION report.
3. Pass REGISTRATION copy to Data Processing Department
4. Keep DEPARTURE copy.

On departure of dog(s):

Kennel Maid to:

1. Complete DEPARTURE form
2. Pass to Data Processing Department

On invoicing:

Accountant to:

1. Accept from computer original and copy INVOICE
2. Confirm total of invoices agrees with total of Day's Takings.
3. Undertake normal debtor's accounting routine.

On receipt of all forms in Data Processing Department:

Cards punched on following basis:

1. One card per dog
2. Format: Owner's name, dog's name, date of booking, arrival date, departure date, daily rate, kennel number.
3. Any irrelevant field to be left blank.
4. Add code for type of card (eg. booking, arrival, etc.)

The program specification

"You know," said Fred, tossing aside his clerical procedures, "I can see that from my forms and files it should be possible to extract my reports, but just how it's done baffles me still."

"Well, that's where the programming and the program specifications part of the systems definition comes in. A *program specification* gathers together all that is required in order that the program can be designed, structured and coded without any further information being needed. By the time the specification is complete it will normally contain a narrative descrip-

---

FRED 'n' FREDA KENNELS   PROGRAM SPECIFICATION - DAYS TAKINGS Program

SUMMARY:
This program produces the DAYS TAKINGS report & at the same time writes an INVOICE tape to be used in the subsequent invoicing of clients
The DAYS TAKINGS report is simply an advisory report on takings, but the INVOICE tape forms the basis of the INVOICING routine providing for that routine the arrival & departure dates, period of kennelling, daily rate and total kennelling charge for each dog - together with a total day's takings figure

NARRATIVE PROGRAM:
Cards punched from day's REGISTRATION & DEPARTURE forms are merged & sorted into NAME order, one card per dog. Then cards are read in conjunction with old TAKINGS master file, and from a comparison of NAMEs the dog is classified as 'arrived' 'departed' or 'still resident'. Dogs arriving are entered on the new TAKINGS master file from the cards, & the details of dogs still resident are rewritten from old to new master file. Dogs departing are omitted from new master file while details of their residence are printed on the DAYS TAKINGS report. These details are also written on the INVOICE tape which is running as part of the program, this tape to be used subsequently in the INVOICING routine

At the end of the run the total takings for the year up to the previous day are read from the end of the old master tape and printed on the DAYS TAKINGS report together with the total takings for the day - the new takings for year-to-date being printed on the report & written on the end of the new master tape. The total takings for the day is also written on the end of the INVOICE tape so that at the end of the INVOICING routine the total value of the invoices can be checked against the total day's takings

RUN FREQUENCY:
Daily.

INPUT:
Old TAKINGS master file (OMF)
Punched cards - REGISTRATIONS & DEPARTUREs merged in NAME order

OUTPUT:
New TAKINGS master file (NMF)
DAYS TAKINGS REPORT
INVOICE tape

MASTER FILE CONTENTS:
Each record - NAME, arrival date, daily rate
At end-of-file - Year's takings to date, coded Z

tion of the program with exact specifications on input, output and file contents. It will also include an outline flow chart of the program and a summary of how that program fits into the over-all system.''

"Right, then — let's have the program specifications for my kennels' system," said Fred.

"I suggest in view of the number of such specifications we look at just one — let's say the DAY'S TAKINGS program," proposed Rufus picking up yet another sheet of paper. "I think it will give you as good an insight as any other.''

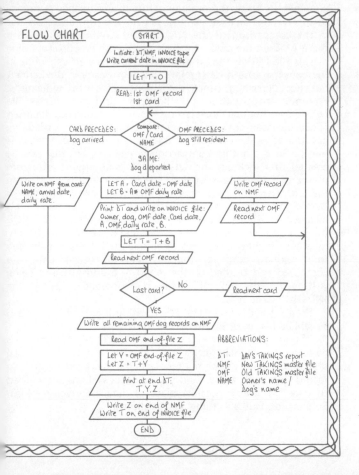

FLOW CHART

START

Initiate: DT, NMF, INVOICE tape
Write current date in INVOICE file

LET T = O

READ: 1st OMF record
1st card

Compare: OMF/Card NAME

CARD PRECEDES: Dog arrived

OMF PRECEDES: Dog still resident

SAME: Dog departed

Write on NMF from card: NAME, arrival date, daily rate.

LET A = Card date - OMF date
LET B = A × OMF daily rate

Write OMF record on NMF

Print DT and write on INVOICE file: Owner, dog, OMF date, Card date, A, OMF daily rate, B.

Read next OMF record

LET T = T + B

Read next OMF record

Last card?   No   Read next card

YES

Write all remaining OMF dog records on NMF

Read OMF end-of-file Z

Let V = OMF end-of-file Z
Let Z = T + V

Print at end DT: T, Y, Z

Write Z on end of NMF
Write T on end of INVOICE file

END

ABBREVIATIONS:

DT   DAY'S TAKINGS report
NMF   New TAKINGS master file
OMF   Old TAKINGS master file
NAME Owner's name / Dog's name

"Looking at the specified input and output," grunted Fred, motioning towards the Input/Output table, "I suspect we'll need tape decks for both the old and the new TAKINGS master files plus one for the INVOICE file, a printer for the DAY'S TAKINGS report and a card-reader." He then turned to look at Rufus's program specification.

"My goodness!" he exclaimed. "Why, this flow chart's complicated enough to be the program itself."

"Nonsense, Fred — though, as I've said, the program specification should be detailed enough to enable the programmer to write the program without any further reference to the systems analyst. As you can see the central feature lies in the comparison of the NAME on the old master file with the NAME on the card. If there's a card with no corresponding master file NAME then it must relate to a new arrival, while in the converse case it must relate to a dog already in the kennels but not departing (since the absence of a card indicates a no-movement situation). If, however, card and master file NAMEs are the same then it must mean that a dog has departed (since they can only be the same if a previously recorded dog has 'moved' — and the only direction such a dog can move is 'out'). So from this comparison a new master file can be created that includes the details of dogs arriving (taken from the cards), the details of dogs still in residence (copied from the old master file, but omitting dogs that have departed) — a DAY'S TAKINGS report relating to the departed animals meanwhile being printed. As a sort of spin-off an INVOICE file is produced recording the arrival and departure dates, daily rates and takings in respect of all departed dogs. Finally, the total takings, both for the day and the year-to-date, are computed and printed on the report — the former also being written on the INVOICE file for subsequent use in the INVOICING routine."

Fred sat and studied the specification long and hard. Then he jabbed his finger in the middle of it.

"Found a flaw," he grinned. "If a dog arrives whose owner's name comes alphabetically after the *last* master file record then you'll have the computer reading a 'next old master file record' that isn't there. And you said the systems analyst had to cater for every possible piece of data, however freakish. So come on Rufus — admit you've slipped."

"Well," replied a rather flustered Rufus, "only to the extent of forgetting to tell you that when the master file is created a fictitious owner, Mr ZZZZ, will be included having a record that ensures his presence neither vanishes nor complicates other aspects of the system other than, perhaps, always appearing inconsequentially at the foot of any other reports utilising the file in their preparation. In that way the computer is prevented from ever coming to the end of the master file before it comes to the end of the cards."

"That's a neat trick," said Fred admiringly.

"I should perhaps warn you that for simplicity the program does not cater for validation — that is (as we saw on your first day) checking to ensure that the input data makes sense. Among other things such validation would make sure, for example, that no card was punched with a wrong departure date."

Rufus then went on to explain that again for simplicity he *hadn't* catered for freakish data — a remark that set Fred intently trying to conceive such data. Before they broke for lunch Rufus had conceded that the system didn't allow for dogs that came and went on the same day, for dogs who were virtually permanently in residence, or for clients who wished to pay when they collected their dogs. He would not, however, concede it failed in respect of a dog that left the day before it arrived.

" 'Freakish' was the word I used," he snapped. "Not downright impossible."

Programming

"And once the system definition is finished I suppose we can start programming, can we?" Fred asked when they resumed after lunch.

"That's right. But the person who does that is, of course, the *programmer*. It's his job to take the program specifications and write in the appropriate language the programs detailed therein. This involves careful, logical thought so that the procedural steps laid down by the systems analyst are converted into program instructions that ensure that the end result envisaged by the analyst is, in fact, realised. He is the person who must make sure that the computer correctly processes each and every piece of information in the manner required."

"As there is already a program specification all written up, does he need to worry much about documentation?" asked Fred.

"My goodness, yes. Indeed, the whole program should be shown in the form of a very detailed flow chart. In addition he will almost certainly make comments in the program itself."

"In the program itself? How do you mean?"

"As the programmer writes out his program he will insert remarks (coded similar to REM in BASIC) such as 'The next 20 instructions ensure that a newly arrived dog is appropriately included in the new TAKINGS master file.' The computer, of course, will ignore such an entry when processing but will reproduce it whenever a printout of the program is requested. This enables anyone trying to follow the program for any reason (such as to maintain, change or update it) to see precisely what is happening at each stage of the program."

"I see. Yes, that would obviously be useful if somebody new wanted to work on the program."

"It's useful, too, for the original programmer," said Rufus drily. "It's astonishing how unintelligible a program can look even to its creator a few months after he's produced it."

Rufus then explained that as an additional safeguard a data-processing department often adopted certain standard methods for documenting programs. These usually included the use of standard forms for certain sections of the documentation and a prescribed method for their use. Thus each programmer who read such documentation would know exactly where to look for specific information irrespective of who wrote it.

Such standard approaches are common in many facets of data-processing and are all aimed at ensuring that the original programmer is not the only person who knows just what the program does. This means other programmers can subsequently work on the program without needing to rely on the presence of the first programmer.

A further advantage that follows from such an approach is that an extra check is placed on the programmer to see that he has considered all aspects of the work in terms of the standards. This helps ensure that no documentation has been omitted or recorded in an incomplete or ambiguous manner.

Operating

"And once we've got the program surely the computer will do the rest," remarked Fred.

"Well, yes — but it will need a little help from the computer operator," answered Rufus. "The *computer operator* is, of course, the person who actually operates the computer. He is the one who loads the magnetic tape reels on to the tape deck and the punched cards into the card-readers, supervises all the peripherals and carries on the constant, if brief, communication with the computer."

"Sounds simple enough," sniffed Fred. "Particularly since the operating system will be over-lording it all."

"Maybe. Certainly the operating system takes much of the mental strain from the operator but for all that he is responsible for expensive machinery (both in terms of capital cost

Fred 'n' Freda Kennels   OPERATING INSTRUCTIONS
                                Daily Routines

1   SWITCH-ON routine: ...

2. BOOKINGS routine: ...

3. DOG LOCATION routine: ...

4. TAKINGS routine: (a) Merge day's REGISTRATIONS and
                           DEPARTURES punched cards.
                      (b) Sort merged cards into NAME order.
                      (c) Load (i) Old TAKINGS master file.
                                (ii) Blank new TAKINGS master file.
                               (iii) Blank INVOICE file.
                                (iv) Sorted cards.
                      (d) Insert blank DAY'S TAKINGS report stationery in
                           duplicate.
                      (e) Run TAKINGS program.
                      (f) Unload all and label.
                      (g) Distribute: (i) Files to Library.
                                      (ii) Cards to Data Processing office.
                                     (iii) Report to: Kennel Manager.
                                                       Accountant.

         On any problems arising, call Fred.

5. Invoicing routine: ...

6. (Fridays only) - Execute weekly routines (see separate sheet).

7. SWITCH-OFF routine: ...

and the cost of operating time) and this does call for qualities of self-reliance and maturity."

"How does he know exactly what to do? Does the operating system tell him everything?"

"Oh, no. It's important that he is given clear, step-by-step instructions as to what he must do when the program is being run. These are called the *operating instructions* and form part of the standard documentation provided by the programmer. If you look among the papers you have there you'll see that I've drafted a possible sequence of operating instructions that might relate to your TAKINGS routine."

And the rest . . .

"Incidentally," Rufus added, "if your installation is at all large you'll also need *librarians* whose job it is to look after all the programs and files and issue them as required to the operator. And, of course, punched card operators if you're going to use punched cards."

"I take it, though," said Fred anxiously, "that the manufacturer will provide me with an engineer to keep the wheels turning?"

"Yes, he will," replied Rufus, wincing at Fred's choice of words.

"And then, of course, I'll need a secretary and a tea-girl," observed Fred thoughtfully. "In fact, come to think of it I'll need them right from the beginning. Better draft an advertisement straight away."

And off went Fred, delighted that he was starting his new job in such a purposeful manner.

8. IMPLEMENTATION

or, how to change horses in mid-data-stream

"I've put in my adverts," said Fred the next day, "and I've told my boss that just as soon as the programs are ready he can ditch the old pen-and-ink method without further ado."

"Then you'd better untell him fast," snapped Rufus. "Such a precipitous abandonment of the established manual procedures is a gratuitous invitation to calamity."

"You mean it would be a little hasty?"

"System implementation, my dear Fred, is something that should be carefully done one stage at a time. Not until you can be absolutely certain that the computer can handle the job competently should you give up any of the manual workings and go 'live', as computer people say. The only good systems in this world are proven systems — and the proving must be thorough and extensive."

"More work," sighed Fred. "All right, then — tell me how to implement a system."

Let's pretend

"The first thing," began Rufus, "is to see what the computer does when faced with some sample input. You know, of course, what it should do but what it actually does may come as a profound revelation to you."

"You give it a day's input, is that the idea?"

121

"Well, at first it's better to create input data — that is, make up examples of the sort of input that will actually be received from the user department."

"You mean make up some typical data?"

"Typical and non-typical. If you're testing a system it is important to test that it can handle the unusual as well as the usual. Indeed, its ability to cope with the unusual is generally a better guide to its quality. Anyway, having prepared your sample input you then put it through the system and check the output against what you expected — and wanted. And this, in a way, forms yet another part of the systems definitions since it again expresses (though in different terms) a relationship between input and output."

"It sounds rather a waste of time playing let's pretend with input data and output," Fred objected.

"We are *not* playing let's pretend — we are simulating the potential actuality," said Rufus haughtily. "But I will admit that the preparation of test data can certainly be a long and tedious job. However, if it's done well it will amply repay the time involved by ensuring that the system does what the user requires it to do. Moreover, such an exercise provides the user with a very clear idea of what the reports from the system will look like while it is still practical to make improving adjustments."

Parallel running

"Well, once the computer's producing the right output from the sample data can you then go 'live'?" asked Fred.

"It would be better, if possible, to have a spell of parallel running first," Rufus advised. "This is where *both* systems, computer and manual, run together but each processing the

data in its own way. Although parallel running results in the same job being done twice over it does mean that if the computer system is deficient in any way the manual results can still be used as normal. Again, the output will be studied to make sure it is what is wanted."

"But if you have to use changed clerical procedures for the computer system won't this mean a great deal of extra work for the user staff?"

"I'm afraid it will. However, this effort is usually well rewarded since not only is the accuracy of the system thoroughly tested in a real-life situation but the user also gains considerable experience of running the new system in circumstances when making mistakes is acceptable."

"But if there isn't the staff for all that?" Fred asked anxiously. "I know our place is grossly under-staffed."

"Well, if you can't have full parallel running what you could do is to select a given period and, as and when they have the time, the user staff reprocess the actual data for the period in terms of the new system. Ultimately the output is checked and the computer's competence confirmed. But the golden rule is always to find time to test however much of a strain this might be. Otherwise it's fairly certain that disaster will strike as soon as the system goes live and everybody is dependent upon it. Indeed, the whole implementation should be taken very carefully with the new computer department showing the user department just how the new system relates to the old one so that preparation for changes in work methods can be phased in gradually over a period leading up to the system going live."

Programming the user

"Yes," said Fred, nodding. "I can well imagine that the personnel in the user departments can create real problems if they fail to follow the procedures properly at their end."

"They can — but they'll have all the procedures fully documented before they start," Rufus reminded him.

"Mm," grunted Fred. "Well, my guess is that all this documentation you've talked about is going to be so extensive that nobody will actually read it."

"That can be a danger," Rufus conceded. "The best way to avoid it is to make sure that there is ample time allowed for training the personnel who will be using the computer system in the way their system works, and also their part in making it successful. This would include taking them through the procedure manuals so that they are aware of exactly what documentation has been provided for them. And with luck, of course, they'll have the chance of using the finalised system in a parallel run before the whole thing goes live."

The computer time-table

"Goes live! That's becoming more and more of a mirage to me," grumbled Fred.

"I think we're about there now," Rufus assured him. "There's usually only one real job left by now — scheduling."

"Scheduling?"

"Yes. As you can imagine, you can't just prepare input data and run programs as and when you feel like it. What you have to do is prepare a time-table showing just when each job will be run — and also the due dates of submission of the input documents from the user departments. Preparing the time-table is

FRED 'n' FREDA KENNELS		DATA SERVICE TIMETABLE MON - SAT		
		FORMS		
		BOOKING CANCELLATION	REGISTRATION	DEPARTURE
MANAGER'S OFFICE	dep	11.00 SX	—	—
KENNEL MAID'S KENNEL	arr	11.10 *		
	dep		21.00 SX	21.00 SX
DATA PROCESSING DEPT. PUNCH ROOM	arr	— 11.10	09.00 SX ‡	09.00 SX ‡
	dep	— 15.00	11.00 SX	13.00 SX
COMPUTER	arr.	— 15.01	11.01 SX	13.01 SX
	dep	— 17.00 RD	15.00 SX RD	15.00 SX RD
MANAGER'S OFFICE	arr.	— 09.00 †		
KENNEL MAID'S KENNEL	arr.	—	15.30 SX	15.30 SX
RD RELATED DOCUMENTS		SX SATURDAYS EXCLUDED		
* FRONT THIRD ONLY		‡ NEXT DAY		

straightforward enough (unless you are short of computer capacity and have to juggle jobs around) but it is important to do it — and equally to see that it's adhered to."

Packages — one man's meat is another man's roast

"It seems to me," said Fred, "that there must be hundreds of computer users in different places all wanting their computer systems to do very much the same thing. I'd say it was rather inefficient to have different computer personnel solving the same old problems over and over again."

"What are you leading up to?" asked Rufus suspiciously.

"Well, wouldn't it be better if, for a given application such as the payroll, a single program could be developed that could be used by anyone wanting to put their payroll on to their computer?"

"Just like you," sighed Rufus. "Trying to dodge the work again. However, there's a great deal in what you say and much time and effort has been directed to preparing what are called *packages*. These are essentially complete, ready-made systems relating to common applications — things like your payroll, sales ledger, purchase ledger, inventory control, production control . . ."

"You're saying I can get complete programs for all these jobs," Fred interrupted excitedly.

"Yes, and more than just the programs. Normally full documentation is included as part of the package — and that in itself, as you'll appreciate, represents a significant saving of effort. And, of course, a further advantage of a package is that it will be debugged and in full working order."

"Marvellous! And where do I get such great wonderful labour-saving devices?"

"Well, independent programming agencies often produce these as do the computer manufacturers. It's a common practice, too, for a manufacturer to arrange for you to use a program developed by another of his customers if that customer agrees."

"Do you buy or rent these packages?"

"Either — although some manufacturers provide them free."

"Right, then," said Fred decisively. "We'll start off with a proven package or two."

Flies in the ointment

"But packages can present problems," Rufus cautioned.

"Problems? What sort of problems?" Fred asked anxiously.

"Problems that arise from the fact that all businesses are different, these differences reflecting themselves in the required computer system," replied Rufus. "Now providing that *your* particular method of working is catered for in the package then your problems will be very few. But once you start moving away from the method of working that the package provides, you can start running into trouble."

"Even so," said Fred, "I would have thought that making a few changes to a proven package would be preferable to starting from scratch."

"I think what you need to consider," remarked Rufus, "is the extent to which the package needs changing. If it has to be changed almost out of recognition then the advantages of a package may be negated because the documentation becomes less relevant, and also because not enough use is made of the established parts of the programs. On the other hand, if you just want to add or remove a couple of fields from a computer report or produce data in a slightly different order then you can probably benefit from adapting a package."

"Even with largish changes I would still have thought tailoring a package would be easier than designing your own program from scratch," Fred persisted. "After all, the adaptation would be a once-and-for-all job and once I'd got it right I'd have it right for good."

"Not so fast," warned Rufus. "Frequently programs need to be altered because of legislative changes. The payroll, for instance, can often require altering to reflect changes in taxation procedure. Now in these sort of circumstances package suppliers often provide an updating procedure, but obviously, if you're going to make large changes in the original package it may prove impossible for you to incorporate the updating procedure in your own system. That means you won't be able to avail yourself of your supplier's services and will have to design and make for yourself all the necessary changes."

How to tailor-make a ready-made system

"If They had any sense," grumbled Fred, "They'd design packages comprehensive enough to suit everybody."

"My dear Fred, you're being impossible now," reproved Rufus. "However, attempts have been made to approach your ideal by writing very general programs which leave the customer to 'fill in the details', as it were, that are peculiar to his business."

"You mean like one of those basic building kits that complete all the really heavy work but let you complete all the other parts of the model any way you want?"

"That's the idea. Some, though, go even further and provide a sort of three-quarters written program with 'plug-in' points where the buyer can add his own pieces of programming routine."

"Rather akin to providing a kitchen with a frame for all the necessary units but leaving it to the customer to provide the actual units he particularly wants?"

"Yes. Anyway by now you'll have realised that there's a considerable number of ways that a package can come to you. I should perhaps add that if it becomes necessary to re-program parts of the package then it becomes essential for the user's staff (or the supplier's staff at some cost to the user) to be thoroughly familiar with the whole system. Otherwise it isn't always possible to deduce what effects making a change in one part of the program might have on the rest of the programs in the package. If this is not correctly evaluated then mayhem can result," declared Rufus decisively.

Reliability

"You know," said Fred nervously, "I can see myself going to enormous trouble to design a system and set it running only to have the computer pack up on me. I should imagine it's virtually impossible to fall back on the old manual methods if there were a major breakdown."

"It certainly is," agreed Rufus. "And if you're going to computerise you'd be very foolish not to make some contingency plans in case of just such a disaster."

"Like?" hinted Fred.

"Well, it's fairly standard practice to arrange some scheme whereby you can use compatible equipment, outside normal hours if required, belonging to the manufacturer or, more likely, another user of the same type of equipment. Mind you, such contingency plans are only necessary if the engineers cannot effect a repair within a reasonable time of the breakdown occurring. I think it's fair to say that relying on a computer system is much less of a risk now than it used to be."

Bureaux — or how to process data without processing data

"I'm glad to hear that," said Fred. "Even so, it's all terribly worrying, this."

"Well, you know, there is a half-way stage where you can have your computer without having a computer."

"Is there then?" exclaimed Fred, pricking up his ears.

"Yes. You can use the services of a *computer bureau*. These bureaux exist by selling time to their clients. There are, naturally, various schemes you can negotiate with such bureaux but typically you tell them the output you want, they tell you the input they need and then you both agree on a fee for them to produce your output from your input. After that you just arrange for them to collect the data on the agreed days and they subsequently deliver your output by agreed deadlines. If you're concerned about the problems of implementing an

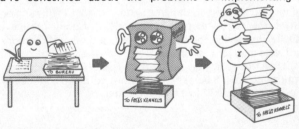

untried major system in a brand-new computer set-up, using a bureau creates a kind of island mid-stream which enables you to make sure you've got your input/output requirements sorted out and a viable set of clerical procedures operating before you take the leap to managing an actual, real, no-nonsense computer."

Rufus detailed the following other advantages of a bureau:

✻ Payment based on actual computer usage. It could be that you only have enough work for a 'part-time' computer in which case the costs of a permanent computer system could very much outweigh the value of the output.

✻ Design by the bureau of tailor-made programs if necessary (though where possible a standard package would be employed).

✻ Removal of responsibility from the user to the bureau for:
  Designing the system
  Operating the computer
  Computer breakdowns

✻ If agreed, preparation by the bureau of input data ready for the computer (e.g. punching the necessary cards).

"Sounds good," said Fred. "But where's the catch?"

"Well, there's no catch really. It is, of course, much more important if you're using a bureau to have your input data ready on time since they will be much less likely to alter their scheduling than your own computer department would. Probably the other biggest disadvantages are that it is usually difficult for the user to obtain extra runs if he requires them, and that little program changes can be expensive — especially if you're running on one of the bureau's standard programs."

"It seems, then, that it saves trouble but at the cost of some flexibility," observed Fred.

"Yes, though a move has been made to make bureau operations more flexible. When worries about flexibility are coupled with concern at the costs involved in collection and distribution it is possible to set up an arrangement whereby the client transmits his input data direct to the bureau's computer via an on-line terminal situated on his own premises. This input is then processed by the bureau's computer in the normal way."

"That should speed up the input side a lot. Can you have the output sent back via the terminal in the same way?"

"Normally these types of terminals are too slow to cope with large volumes of print but if you want you can install a fast printer. Such printers, however, usually require a mini-CPU to control their operations — when the whole system is referred to as a *remote job entry* station (*RJE*). Actually, having gone this far it normally pays to add a punched card or paper-tape reader — after which the unit can be regarded as being virtually a computer in its own right, which, however, relies on another, bigger, computer to carry out the heavier processing work."

"Amazing," remarked Fred.

Fred sums up

"It seems to me," said Fred, leaning back and looking thoughtfully at the ceiling, "that there are three ways I can get a job done by computer. I can design the whole system from scratch with all the documentation and programming that involves, or I can buy a package which, while perhaps less flexible in terms of output, does save me from worrrying about system design and programming so I can concentrate on organising the clerical side, or I can use a bureau which will save me design, programming, computer operating and a large degree of responsibility — though with the added inflexibility of more rigid schedules."

"In a nutshell," confirmed Rufus.

"I suppose I can mix them, can't I?" Fred asked looking at Rufus. "I mean, use a bureau while I'm waiting for my computer to be delivered and get some experience of the clerical problems. Then, when it arrives, use packages for the common and typical routines while designing my own systems for the special and untypical work?"

"Both allowable and admirable."

"You know, I think I'll be able to get a very decent system ticking over one day," said Fred confidently.

". . . If I live long enough," he added cautiously.

9. TIME SHARING

or, how to have a cosy chat with your computer

"The computer's running beautifully," remarked Fred cheerfully some months later.

"So all your problems have disappeared, then," said Rufus.

"Well, no — not quite all. There's still one thing that's giving me a bit of a headache. You see, when the managers heard that I'd a successful computer installation under way they began to want me to tell them things such as the optimum production batch size and the effect on the capital structure in five years time of sales increasing at differing annual rates. Now, they know exactly how to get the answer they want — all they require from me is the computing facilities."

"And, of course, you've found that it is grossly uneconomic to do and very disruptive of your crucial scheduling of the routine work."

"How did you know that?" asked a surprised Fred.

Interactive facilities — or chatting up the computer

"It's very common," replied Rufus. "Unfortunately, though, there's no simple solution. The fact is that your particular computer is just not suitable for this kind of 'personal' service. What your managers need is a method whereby manager and computer *interact* — that is, talk to each other."

"But computers can't talk," Fred objected.

"By 'talk' I mean 'converse'. The idea here is that the manager specifies a particular situation — such as a list of proposed daily kennel rates and a forecasted level of kennel demand at these rates. The computer then tells him the consequential effects if that situation materialises — such as your daily takings. If these effects are not satisfactory then the manager changes one or more factors in the situation and asks the computer for a revised result."

"So if the daily takings weren't enough I could try again with increased daily rates, could I?"

"Or decreased rates and increased demand, yes."

"Repeating the whole business, I suppose, as often as necessary to find the combination of rates and demand that gives me the best takings," said Fred thoughtfully. "And that you call 'interactive'?"

"That's right. And, as you can imagine, if a manager had the *sole* use of your computer until he'd obtained his final answer there'd be a totally unacceptable loss of computer running time."

"I suspect we need some kind of multiprogramming here," ventured Fred.

"More than that. We need a system whereby the computer is shared between *users* rather than just between programs as in the case of multiprogramming."

"But wouldn't that mean the users would have to keep queueing up for their turn? I don't think they'd like that much."

"No problem there, Fred," Rufus assured him. "Almost always the computer moves so fast that it can do the work for all the users in less time than it takes any one of them to read his answer. We call this *time-sharing*. As you'll appreciate, one of the greatest advantages of time-sharing is that the user can work entirely at his own pace."

"It's just what we need," said Fred enthusiastically. "Can I adapt my computer for time-sharing?"

"Well, unless you have a considerable demand for this sort of technique it's frankly not worth doing yourself. There are plenty of outside agencies that provide this service and, as we saw when we talked about how a computer worked in our early discussions, all you need is a terminal and a telephone line and you can have a direct link to their computers."

"Seems a bit like having a dog and paying someone else's to bark for you," objected Fred.

"Yet people with cars still fly inter-city," Rufus pointed out. "By the way, let me just say in passing that in time-sharing the users are all working with *different* programs — they are not merely using a common program and data file, as they would be if they were different stores locations concerned with stocks in a central store."

"Is that significant?"

"It has relevance if you want to distinguish time-sharing from real-time computing — which, no doubt, we'll discuss one day."

Time-sharers all

Rufus then went on to explain that the user of a time-sharing system was likely to be someone who wanted a rapid response to a definable problem usually involving considerable computation — typically an engineer or a draughtsman. A research worker might be more concerned with mathematical models or calculating sales forecasts. In the field of education the computer terminal enables the teacher to allow a school class to use a computer as a problem-solving tool, so giving them first-hand experience of the flexible power that a computer can offer.

"Mainly theoreticians, by the sound of it," snorted Fred.

"Originally this was so," replied Rufus. "However, recently there's been a significant increase in the number of business users adopting time-sharing. As you yourself have found, there's a demand for production planning and financial projections that cannot easily be met by using the company's computer, but can be met by using time-sharing. As a matter of fact one of the areas where the technique can prove of considerable help is the preparation of simple routine reports incorporating small volumes of figure input."

"Routine reports? How does that come about?"

"Well, have you ever considered how such a report is built up? First, the figures have to be collected and then consolidated into the actual entries. After this totals have to be calculated — often across rows as well as down columns — and any ratios worked out. Sometimes comparative figures are included and the differences between these and the actual figures need to be found. Finally the whole of the report has to be typed out — in standard layout. Now look at the scope for error if all this is done manually — quite apart from the time demand."

"You can use a terminal to do that?"

"Of course. It's just a matter of writing a program detailing how the figures are to be put together — and what totals and differences are required. Then each time the report is needed all one has to do is to list the basic figures for the period and run the program. And the end result will be a typed-out, error-free report presented only seconds later. Look — here's the sort of thing it could produce for your kennels just from an input of fourteen figures." And Rufus showed Fred a possible Weekly Boarding Report.

FRED'N'FREDA: WEEKLY BOARDING REPORT

DAY	LITTLE DOGS AT £0.85 PER DAY			BIG DOGS AT £1.25 PER DAY			TOTAL			CAPACITY UTILISATION (100% = 78 KENNELS)	RATIO LITTLE/BIG DOGS
	NO.	%DAILY AVERAGE	EARNINGS £	NO.	%DAILY AVERAGE	EARNINGS £	NO.	%DAILY AVERAGE	EARNINGS £		
MON	44	104	37.40	22	92	27.50	66	100	64.90	85	2.0
TUE	48	114	40.80	25	104	31.25	73	110	72.05	94	1.9
WED	33	78	28.05	30	125	37.50	63	95	65.55	81	1.1
THU	36	85	30.60	21	88	26.25	57	86	56.85	73	1.7
FRI	31	74	26.35	20	83	25.00	51	77	51.35	65	1.6
SAT	52	123	44.20	24	100	30.00	76	115	74.20	97	2.2
SUN	51	121	43.35	26	108	32.50	77	116	75.85	99	2.0
TOTAL	295		250.75	148		210.00	463		460.75		
DAILY AVERAGE	42.1		35.82	24.0		30.00	66.1		65.82	85	1.76
DAILY TARGET	48		40.80	30		37.50	78		78.30	100	1.6
ACTUAL AS % OF DAILY TARGET	88		88	80		80	85		84		

"Yes. Well, I can see that this sort of application would help any manager involved in handling data, but would it help, say, the salesman or the auditor?"

"Oh, yes. It could help the salesman, for example, by allowing him to test from a customer's specification which model from a large range is best suited to that customer's needs. And it can help the auditor by, say, generating independently of the client random numbers to decide which items to sample and also by enabling him to operate on a control audit file from his client's premises or from his own offices."

"You mean, from a terminal set up in the auditor's own office?" asked Fred in surprise.

"Yes. Don't forget that in size and appearance it's hardly any different from a teleprinter — though many have a paper tape punch-cum-reader attached to them. They used to have a very low printing speed, but the development of terminals with faster printing devices is alleviating this problem. Also it is becoming more and more possible to program from a visual display unit which speeds things up since such a unit can display output much faster than it can be printed."

How terminals can communicate

"The way you are talking there appears to be no problems whatsoever in having a terminal anywhere you want it," said Fred rather sceptically.

"Well, there aren't really," replied Rufus. "In fact, I think it's fair to say that there are none at all as far as the slower terminals are concerned. As long as you've a telephone you can have a terminal."

"Does it need to be specially 'wired in' to the 'phone?" Fred asked.

"Good heavens, no. You can have a portable terminal if you want, though you'll need a small additional piece of equipment in the form of an *acoustic coupler* whose function is to convert the terminal signals into sound — and vice versa. To operate the user simply dials the computer of his choice on the telephone and places the telephone handset in the acoustic coupler. This enables the handset to pick up the signals and pass them down the line to the computer — and, similarly, in reverse take the computer reply and turn it into terminal signals."

"It sounds, then, as if you can take your terminal to any part of the world you want."

"If you wish you can. One major company in particular has taken advantage of modern communication equipment to provide a world-wide service available to the user for a communication cost of no more than the price of a local telephone call to whichever connection centre is nearest to him. From this connection centre his call passes through a series of land-lines (and trans-oceanic cables or communication satellite

where necessary) to a machine centre in the United States where several different computers are available for his use."

"That's impressive, but is it useful?" asked Fred.

"Well, it certainly has the advantage to the user that there is a very wide range of packages and standard programs held in the centre that he can use. In addition, users can exchange their programs with other users by mutual agreement. You can also imagine the scope and advantages of such an arrangement to international organisations. It enables them, for instance, to maintain files in one place that can be used by the whole multi-national corporation thus ensuring truly up-to-date information. It also enables these organisations to follow standard practices in, say, the presentation of accounting information by the use of common programs."

Fred wants to do it

"You make it sound all very simple," said Fred. "But if I wanted to do it I bet it would take weeks of training."

"Nonsense," replied Rufus. "You know how to write a simple BASIC program from our earlier conversations. All you have to do is use the terminal is type out your program, conclude with the word RUN and out will come the answer."

"What if I write the program incorrectly?"

"Don't worry — the terminal will tell you if you do that."

"But will I have to write out the whole program again?"

"No, not at all. Just retype any erroneous instructions. And as long as you've remembered to number your instructions leaving large gaps then if you've omitted some necessary instruction all you do is select one of the free numbers in an appropriate gap and type the additional instruction."

"But it will be out of order if it's typed at the end of the program," Fred protested.

"Not really. Your instruction number ensures that your instruction is put in the correct instruction box and therefore is read in the correct sequence."

"Of course! Right then — let's have a shot at it."

"Very well," agreed Rufus. "We'll walk over to the Departmental terminal and you can see how you get along."

Fred logs in

"The first thing," said Rufus having sat Fred down in front of the terminal, "is to *log in* — that is, initiate the contact and go through the identification procedure."

"Surely I just ring the computer up," remarked Fred, and looking at the telephone number displayed on the wall above him, dialled the computer. He was rewarded with a high-pitched whistle.

"That's the computer answering," explained Rufus, "telling you to put the handset in the acoustic coupler."

As Fred shut the coupler lid the terminal sprang to life and typed the date and time.

"That's a standard message," explained Rufus. "Confirming that contact has been made and welcoming you on-line."

Underneath the date and time the computer then typed USER CODE.

"Hm," muttered Fred, and, ignoring this cryptic remark, typed the first line of his program.

"ILLEGAL ENTRY," said the terminal.

Fred typed his program line again.

"ILLEGAL ENTRY," repeated the terminal.

"But there's nothing wrong with my program," cried Fred despairingly to Rufus.

"Nothing at all," confirmed Rufus. "But under the procedure the first thing you must do is type in the correct user code. You see, Fred, it's very easy for anyone to get access to a terminal so it's essential for security reasons that the terminal

operator proves to the computer that he's a bona fide user —
and, indeed, which user he is." As he spoke Rufus leant over
Fred and typed in his user number UNIT 99.

"Not only does that identify you to the computer," he
continued, "but it also enables you to call on any permanent
file that is indexed under that code."

"I see," said Fred, "so that stops any other user using a
different code from ever getting hold of your file — even
though he's sharing the same computer with you?"

"That's the idea, though the user can specify that other
designated users can have access to his files. Usually, though,
in such a case he will instruct the computer to allow other
users only to *read* his files and restrict any changes to himself.
Some systems have a PASSWORD entry as a double security
check. The main advantage is that if it seems that the user
code and password have become known to unauthorised users
then changing the password re-establishes security without
having to alter the user code — and all the referencing that is
associated with the user code and the user's files."

Fred looked at the terminal again and saw that it had
typed USER CHARGE CODE whilst they had been talking.

"Not another code," groaned Fred.

"Of minor importance. You can put whatever you want
there actually, but the idea behind it is that when the computer bills you for your time, the invoice will be broken down
to show just how much is charged against each code you have
entered. Again, some systems have it and some don't. Tell you
what, why not enter 'FRED' here and then we'll know just
how much this session with you will have cost us."

So Fred typed FRED and the terminal replied READY.

"About time," grunted Fred, and he began to type his
BASIC program.

How the computer does it

A couple of hours later an impressed Fred accompanied
Rufus back to his study.

"Clever stuff, this," he admitted. "Can you tell me how it's
done?"

"As you suspected at the beginning, it's essentially an
extended form of multiprogramming," replied Rufus. "Predict-
ably, the operating system plays a large part in things — includ-

ing handling the software that controls the terminal. So the initial contact is between the terminal user and the operating system. It is the operating system that takes you through the log-in procedure and then allocates the necessary resources to handle your program. It also arranges to run your program when you type the word 'RUN'."

"I rather feel that allocating resources is a somewhat different matter in time-sharing than in my computer system."

"It is. In your system the object is to process a job as quickly as possible so as to release the computer resources for other work. The important thing about a time-sharing system serving many users is that at any time the system is responsible for a great many jobs, all partially completed and most likely to be waiting for a user at a terminal to take some action. As these programs between them would probably fill the memory several times over if included in full, very effective use must be made of the memory. This means rigid control of the time that a program is in memory and an efficient way of swapping programs and data between core store and the discs providing a back-up store."

"I suspect a user musn't be allowed to feed in an indefinite amount of stuff, in that case," remarked Fred.

"No, he's given limits, all right. But you can't make the limits too stringent or the advantages of a terminal start to be eroded away."

"Could you use the technique we looked at when we talked about multiprogramming — having the programs in sittings?"

"Yes, that's the approach."

"I must say I find this business of pushing programs around all over the place a little alarming. I mean, what happens if the computer breaks down in the middle of it all?"

"Well," replied Rufus, "you could, of course, lose the information you were working on at the time but most systems provide facilities which minimise the inconvenience caused. When the user at the terminal is entering either lines of program or lines of data the system writes these lines into what is called a *work file*. This is essentially a file using disc storage that contains all the details relating to whatever program you are working on at the time. If the computer breaks down and the information in memory is lost then all the data up to the beginning of the interrupted run can be recovered from the work file."

Command Language

"As a matter of interest I should tell you," Rufus continued, "that there are quite a few commands that you can give that relate to the work file specifically. For instance, at the beginning of a time-sharing session the terminal user can either type 'LOAD' and load the contents of an existing file held by the computer into this work file (that is transfer the data in a permanent file to the work file), or type 'MAKE' and make a new program and set of data which will be entered in the work file specifically."

"I like the word 'command' that you used just now," said Fred happily. "It makes me feel I am the master — and I have as a servant a very powerful genie."

"That is definitely part of the appeal of a good time-sharing system," remarked Rufus. "These commands form a little language of their own. They don't, as it happens in the case of the other languages we discussed, instruct the CPU what to do with the *data* presented when an instruction is reached in the course of running a program, but instead instruct the *computer* what to do as an over-all machine *at the moment the command is typed.* So RUN means 'run *now* the program in

the work file' and LOAD, MAKE, SAVE and LIST are, of course, also part of the command language as in the GOODBYE which I typed when we'd finished with the terminal."

"GOODBYE, then, I take it, is the command terminating the session and dismissing one's servant?"

"That's right."

"You know, that's about the most useful command of all, isn't it?" observed Fred. "Short, sweet and to the point. GOODBYE, Rufus." And Fred was gone.

"Insolent young puppy," growled Rufus, but as the clock showed it was opening time there was little condemnation in his voice.

10. HOW TO KEEP
YOUR DATA UP TO DATE
or, real-time and all that

"Who'd be a Data Processing Manager if he had any choice?" remarked Fred, weeping bitterly into his beer.

"More problems?" asked Rufus sympathetically.

"Of course. It's the Production Controller now. Says my reports detailing stock levels are so out-of-date that they're useless. And he gets the previous day's closing balances by early afternoon at the latest. And to make it worse he claims that the computer can do the work in plenty of time — it's me who's to blame for the delay."

"So it is — or, more accurately, it's the system. You're using what is called a *batch processing* method which entails collecting the information, punching that information into cards and then gathering together a batch of such cards for processing — and all before the computer even starts! Then, of course, the printed output has to be delivered to the user. All this takes time — too much time, sometimes, for users who need to know the precise up-to-date position when making decisions. Apart from production control such up-to-date information would be crucial, for example, to airlines when accepting bookings for aircraft seats — or, indeed, as it might be to your kennels."

"Well, I'm not going to stop everything I'm doing every time a stores issue note comes in, just so that he can have his stock record file updated there and then," declared Fred firmly.

"No, I agree. If you're using a batch processing system then it is quite impractical. Frankly, I feel there's no alternative but for your Production Controller to use a different system."

"Like what?" asked Fred.

Fred meets real-time

"Like a real-time system," replied Rufus. "In a *real-time system* the record files are updated at virtually the same moment as events actually occur. So the BOOKINGS master file in your kennels business would be updated the moment a booking was made."

"You mean a card is punched and shoved into the computer there and then?" asked an incredulous Fred.

"Faster than that. The booking clerk would, in fact, have a terminal so that he could enter the booking data as he made the booking."

"That means the BOOKINGS file would need to be continuously on tap."

"It does. But that's not the end, of course. Indeed, the whole point of a real-time system is that the smack-up-to-date file record is instantly available to whoever needs the data. Therefore equipment such as visual display units are linked to the computer and are able to display any requested information. Making such a request is known as 'interrogating the computer'."

"It sounds very much the same as on-line to me."

'Well, of course, the terminal and VDU *are* on-line. But the term 'on-line' relates to hardware and simply means electrically connected to the processor while 'real-time' refers to a system whereby the user can have operations performed at the same moment as a piece of data is received."

"So it's the same as time-sharing," concluded Fred, who was determined that real-time should be the same as something or other.

"Again, yes, up to a point. But in time-sharing each user has his own programs and his own files and he alone alters them whereas in a real-time system there can be a hundred or more users utilising the same programs and *all operating on the same file* and changing the file information. Also in time-sharing the

emphasis is usually on making computations — the files remaining relatively unchanged — whereas in real-time a major feature of the system is the *alteration of the file data* — sometimes second by second. In fact, the best illustration of a real-time system is probably the one I've already given of the seat reservation system employed by airlines."

Real-time and updating

"What if two different airline booking clerks were both advised that just one place was available on a flight and both their customers took up that one seat?" asked Fred.

"Or two storekeepers, both being told at the same time that there were three tyres in stock, and both decided to take all three," added Rufus. "Yes, that certainly is a problem that can arise. In theory, of course, the answer is easy — don't let the second user have the information until the first user

has made his decision and the record has been updated. However, whilst this can certainly be done in the case of small systems, it can become an expensive computer operation when there are, say, 100 terminals since each time a terminal wants a piece of information it may well need a program that checks through all the remaining terminals to ensure no others are using that particular record. Such a program is based on searching a table held in memory."

When all is lost

"Yes, I see that can be quite a problem," said Fred thoughtfully. "But I should think it's nothing to the problem that arises when, in the middle of all this continuous updating, the confounded machine breaks down."

"Ah, yes — that *is* a tricky one," conceded Rufus. "Particularly since it is obviously totally impractical and uneconomic to have the computer handle only one message at a time from start to finish. Clearly, at any moment a number of separate messages will be in process and being handled simultaneously. Moreover, each message can be at any one of many program steps. Consequently, if the computer breaks down it will not just be one record that is lost at some unknown step in the process but perhaps twenty or thirty."

"Which makes the situation considerably worse, then," observed Fred. "What's more, if you're using a real-time system how can you possibly have everybody wait while you untangle the inevitable snarl-up and get all the files correct and up-to-date once more?"

"It is difficult," Rufus confessed, "and it requires a special and comprehensive system — called a *recovery system* — designed to do just that. The system is, like the operating system, a permanent and immediately available *program*. As you would imagine, the basic principle in such a program is to 'make a note' of everything that happens as the processing goes along so that the whole day's run can be re-created if need be and the state of the record immediately prior to the breakdown re-established."

"*Everything*?" gasped Fred.

"Well, everything of relevance to any necessary recovery. The two primary pieces of information relate to messages and file records that have been altered. In the case of messages, each incoming message is given a serial number and both message and eventual reply are noted. In the case of the file records, each record altered is noted in its 'before' and 'after' forms."

"When you say the system 'makes a note' do you mean it types out the note on the console?"

"Goodness, no. Quite apart from such a procedure being impossibly slow the resulting output would need to be interpreted by people — and they'd take far too long to put things right. No, the object of a recovery system is to enable the computer to make the necessary recovery itself — automatically and quickly. So it 'makes a note' on a magnetic tape which is usually referred to as a *log tape*. The log tape, then, will record in chronological order every critical stage in the processing of all messages and answers passing through the system, and every change in the files. So as you'll appreciate the computer can, if need be, re-create all the day's happenings in no more time than it takes to read the tape."

"Which will be much faster than I could read the console output," admitted Fred.

How a computer recovers

"All right," continued Fred. "The computer's just broken down, we've lost everything that was in the core store and all hell is let loose. Now, just how does the computer put itself right?"

"Well," replied Rufus, "there are a number of different techniques. Perhaps the most obvious one is to run the log tape *backwards*, resetting all the files at their 'before' states until it reaches the point where all the lost core store material related to operations subsequent to that point in time. Then reversing the log tape and running it forward will have the effect of re-enacting all the events up to the breakdown moment — and so put us in the identical situation that we were in when everything was lost."

"It sounds very tortuous, all this running backwards and forwards and setting and re-setting everything. Isn't there an easier way?"

"It depends. If all terminal inputs can be temporarily stopped a *check-point* technique can be adopted. This involves stopping all the incoming messages at appropriate moments and waiting until replies to all prior messages have been sent so that no uncompleted work remains in the system. If the check-point time is recorded on the log tape and if the system is designed to embody the updating time in each record updated then recovery can be based on re-creating the records between the last check-point time and the moment of breakdown."

"What if your log tape was involved in the breakdown?"

"Ah, well now, in practice you'd be writing your log on both tape *and* disc simultaneously. So you'd use the disc copy."

"But your discs could have broken down too," Fred insisted.

"Then you'll have further disc copies," snapped Rufus. "But, Fred, you must appreciate that on this business of recovery it is theoretically possible to recover from *any* situation. So rather than think about the 'how' of recovery you should be thinking about the effect of a breakdown in your particular business and the advantages and disadvantages of all the potential recovery techniques at your disposal."

Real-time and hardware

"You know," said Fred, "what with operating systems, recovery systems, compilation, assembly, error correction and so on I'm getting the impression that actual data-processing occupies only an insignificant fraction of the time, effort and cost of maintaining the overall data-processing system."

"But my dear Fred, in any system — manual or otherwise — that involves data the actual business of processing the data

is small compared with that of organising the processing and seeing that it is done efficiently, economically, in good time and free from errors," Rufus pointed out.

"Maybe. But I must say that when it comes to operating real-time I wonder if it's worth all the effort," said Fred. "It must take years to program such a system and that, I imagine, will make it very expensive."

"It does," admitted Rufus. "But there are situations where effective processing is impossible without such a fast response system — such as the seat-booking operation we've referred to. However, the cost of programming has long been recognised as a problem and as the use of real-time systems has increased computer manufacturers have modified their hardware to do things which previously had to be done by the programming. For instance, the problem of stopping a second user from working with a record already being handled can now be solved by attaching a piece of hardware to the disc equipment which notes the location of any record being accessed so as to block any other attempts to access the same record. Other developments in hardware have been directed towards enabling the machine itself to correct some of its own failings. In cases where hardware is involved and cannot be self-correcting (for instance, magnetic tape drives) the hardware and software together test and monitor performance and log and analyse the information so that engineers can see if any attention is required."

"It seems to me," said Fred, "that if the hardware is watched so carefully the system should never fail."

"Well, the system can fail even if there's nothing wrong with the hardware," cautioned Rufus. "Sometimes the *software* itself cannot cope with some particular combination of events."

"Such as?"

"Such as when an internal error correction coincides with a heavy processing load."

"What happens then?"

"It depends. It often takes considerable analysis to determine what the combination of events was. However, since it's unlikely that that combination will arise again, one usually just re-starts the machine and hopes for the best."

"It's still stopped for a while, though, isn't it?"

"True. And that can prove inconvenient. But there is only one way of ensuring that a computer system will keep running all the time and that's to have two similar computer systems or, alternatively a *duplex configuration* which is a single system having two of every unit where only one is required," answered Rufus. "The decision to have two separate systems or a duplex system will depend upon individual requirements and particularly how long it is feasible to be without the system. If it is possible to be without service for, say, half an hour, then there is probably ample time to move all work from the collapsed system to the standby system by manually transferring the discs and tapes."

"And what if it's not possible to be without service for half an hour?" asked Fred belligerently.

"Well, in that case inter-communication between the systems is essential. One possibility is sharing the disc files by linking them to both systems. This would allow either system immediate access to the data — which is the most important requirement — and this, together with some mechanism for automatically switching the communication lines, would allow the service to continue with minimal interruption (say five minutes). As usual, the crucial resources are a processor (CPU) and memory and the point about a duplex configuration is that the system is capable of sharing its work between two processors. If one fails the other carries on, though obviously providing only a reduced capacity."

"As a matter of fact," continued Rufus warming to his theme, "the principle of duplication can be extended to all electrical connecting paths and units in the system, with the hardware automatically trying an alternative electrical path if the first fails, or taking data from an alternative disc unit holding copies of files normally obtained from the disc it cannot access."

"It all sounds like money to me," muttered Fred.

"I'm afraid it is. Although electronic circuitry is increasingly reliable there does seem to be no alternative at the moment to duplication in those cases where continuity of service is of prime importance."

"Can you never have complete reliability for any unit?"

"Not yet. No matter how well-monitored your hardware, some unanticipated failing is bound to occur sooner or later. And in the recognition of this probability many of the operating systems prepared by the computer manufacturers now contain aids to recovery (such as automatically maintaining two disc files) so that the user is covered as far as is practical against computer failure."

"You know," said Fred after a thoughtful pause, "I don't think that the information required by our Production Controller really justifies the cost of a real-time system."

"My dear Fred, you mustn't jump to conclusions," reproved Rufus sternly. "Why, the whole business of reporting stock levels using a real-time system screams out for a feasibility study."

"Feasibility study, my eye," retorted Fred, turning to leave. "My lads have quite enough to do without any of that nonsense."

Which just went to show how far Fred's experience as a Data Processing Manager had developed his ability to make quick and effective decisions. And how little he subsequently intended to draw on Rufus' extensive know-how.

Which suited Rufus.

11. QUO VADIS?

As it happened some six months later Fred was having a drink at his local, the "Ferry Boat", when in walked Rufus. After a welcome which included an unflattering allusion to a Scotch egg, Fred led Rufus to his own favourite corner.

"You're doing well, I hear," remarked Rufus putting down his gin after the customary salutations.

"Had another rise, yes," Fred replied complacently. "Things are going nicely now. Still, I sometimes wonder where all this computer business will finish up!"

"Yes, the computer world is one that changes with considerable rapidity."

"My trouble is that with the old nose to the grindstone every day I've no time to look around to see what's happening," Fred confessed. "Can you bring me up to date a bit?"

A computer by any other name . . .

"Well," remarked Rufus, "it's very much a matter of more and more of less and less."

"Not the first today, is it?" muttered Fred.

"I made what is referred to as a 'paradoxical remark'," Rufus explained stuffily. "What I meant was that with the advent of the microchip it has been very much a matter of developing more and more components that take up progressively less and less space. This means that computers are now becoming so small that they can be fitted comfortably into a whole variety of relatively small-scale equipment."

"Like?" prompted Fred.

"Like cash registers, washing machines and wrist watches. Even," Rufus continued, nodding across the room at a couple of things from outer space, "pub games."

"You mean that Wroosh-Bong is a computer? But where's the tape-deck and printer? And how do I get my data in?"

"My dear Fred, don't be so unimaginative. Can't you see that you have a VDU instead of a printer and that your data is directly input via the control knobs?"

"That my data is in effect the information I'm giving the gizmo as to where I want my space-rocket to be?" said Fred thoughtfully. "Yes, but that still doesn't make it a computer any more than my bicycle's a computer. Just like my bike — it responds to my manual control."

"Rubbish, Fred. That gizmo, as you call it, not only displays the movement of your spaceship but also tests if it is in a force field that will destroy it — and if it is, to depict its cataclysmic dissolution. There is, in fact, quite a sophisticated program in there."

"Surely," mused Fred reflectively, "isn't that what they call a microprocessor rather than a computer?"

Rufus shrugged his shoulders.

"Words, Fred, words. A microprocessor *is* a computer. A special purpose one albeit, but nevertheless still a computer."

"When is a computer not a computer?" riddled Fred.

"When it can't decide," replied Rufus quickly. "As long as the gizmo (useful word of yours, that, Fred) can compare one piece of information with another and automatically select one of an alternative set of responses as a result of that comparison then by today's terminology it probably justifies the title 'computer' — even if it doesn't look like one. But, frankly, this is all academic. The distinction between computers and many other things these days is becoming rapidly more and more blurred. Better to look at the applications that have followed the computer revolution."

Nearer and clearer

"And what's cooking in that direction?" asked Fred.

"Well, the emphasis is now being placed on cutting out the human 'middleman' of data — in other words, on getting the computer nearer and nearer the source of its input while providing the output nearer and nearer the point where it's needed."

"Your data untouched by human hand, sort of thing."

"As far as possible, yes. For instance, they're putting terminals more and more on to shop-floors of factories so that production data is inputed on the spot."

"But blast-furnacemen aren't terminal operators," protested Fred.

"Primarily, no. So that means the system has to be designed to minimise what they have to do. As a result such terminals are made with the ability to read a punched card (carrying, say, the job number and material input details) and a magnetic badge (to identify the person operating the furnace) as well as having a keyboard (for entry of blast times and other on-the-spot details)."

"They'll need to be pretty tough, too," growled Fred.

"They are," Rufus assured him. "And a further example of this sort of trend is the bank cash dispenser. Not only do they dispense cash but they can also update the customer's account simultaneously."

"A real-time application, eh?"

"That's right. And by giving every branch a terminal linked to the Head Office computer it is possible for a manager at any branch to obtain a fully up-to-date record of any customer's account."

"Handy if I need to draw a few Fredsticks when I'm visiting Zed," said Fred. "Well, that's industry and finance being served. What about the distributive trades?"

A computer on every counter

"As a matter of fact that's where the application potential is greatest," replied Rufus. "Particularly in the retail shop."

"What — the old corner general stores?" grinned Fred.

"Could be, one day. But for the moment developments are restricted mainly to the larger self-service outlets. As you will appreciate, Fred, every day thousands and thousands of hours are spent by girls at check-out counters reading the prices on items and ringing up the sales on cash registers."

"Yes, I take your point exactly. I've often thought that if a punched card were to be attached to the packet . . . ."

"You're behind the times, Fred. These days there's a device called a *light pen* which is used to read such data."

"A logical function for a pen," remarked Fred sarcastically.

"This data," continued Rufus, oblivious to Fred's comment, "can be in the form of printed vertical lines on the price tag. The pen, which is connected to the computer, is passed across these lines and 'reads' them as a series of pulses — and by designing the spacing between them so as to code these pulses, the computer is able to both display the price on, and enter it into, the cash-out register."

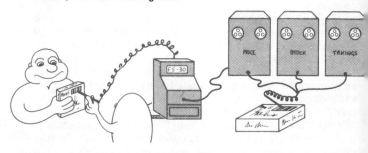

"Fantastic," sniffed Fred. "But what happens if the tag falls off?"

" There are times, Fred, when, as a destructive critic there is no-one to equal you. But, I'll admit for once you've put your finger on a potentially serious defect."

"So for your next trick . . . ." murmured Fred.

"So the next development has been to omit the price from the tag and have instead only a coded product identification number. And this number enables the computer to identify the current price to be notified to the register. Moreover, it also enables the stock records to be updated on a real-time basis as well as other records involving the product. And this, of course, considerably assists in the management of the store."

"But the tag can *still* fall off," Fred insisted.

"Ah, but you see, Fred, they arrange it now so that the manufacturer of the products *prints the line code on the product wrapper* — as part of the product label."

"But, but . . ." stuttered Fred, "surely different stores will have different codes. The manufacturer can't print special labels for each of his customers."

Rufus waved Fred's objection aside.

"Nothing that a bit of standardisation can't sort out," he said airily.

"You mean that every code could, say, be a two-part code — the first part being a code number given by the trade association to the manufacturer and the second part the product code set by the manufacturer himself — which he'd advise to all his customers?" Fred suggested after giving the matter a little thought.

"The details are unimportant. The thing is that there's no real difficulty about the application."

Processing the Word

"For all that, a computer still can't write a convincing letter to my tax inspector," bemoaned Fred.

"The ability to give credence to an impossible scenario is a creative act still beyond the powers of the computer," conceded Rufus. "Nevertheless, computers can very much assist in the physical act of writing. In that capacity they are termed *word processors.*"

"I use a pen myself."

"And produce a flawless letter free from all spelling and grammatical errors, needing no inserted after-thoughts or tactful deletions, and with the argument flowing logically and persuasively — first time around?"

"Never," moaned Fred. "If I start once I start a dozen times."

"Throwing away and then having to recopy each time the bits that were just as you wanted them?"

"Well, of course. Can't cut them out and paste 'em onto the next try, can I?"

"With a word processor you can in effect do just that. The machine is essentially a VDU which displays what you've typed. But being electronic the insertion and deletion of letters, spaces, sentences and paragraphs can be effected at the touch of a key. Indeed, sentences and paragraphs can be moved from one place to another. And no need to worry about fitting the words into a line — any respacing or movement of words to different lines to compensate for insertions and deletions is all automatic."

"And when you've got it right you press a button and it types it all out?"

"Yes. Moreover, if you want to use a letter or suchlike more than once it can be stored in any of the usual ways and once again at the touch of a key it will be produced. Or you could first alter or update certain portions if you wished."

"Will it put letters into their envelopes?"

"As yet, no."

"Rather limited repertoire, hasn't it?" sniffed Fred.

Computers and data communications

"Mind you, with modern developments letters in envelopes may well soon be obsolete," remarked Rufus, and seeing Fred's puzzled look continued, "After all, there's no reason why one word processor shouldn't be connected to another so that the processed letter (or perhaps memo) on the first is displayed on the VDU of the second — as and when required."

"A sort of TV teleprinter coupled to a kind of answering service, eh?" reflected Fred. "But isn't that more a matter of communications rather than computers?"

"It is. But frankly if it's the future you're looking to, then it's the conjunction of computers with communications that you should concentrate on. You have doubtless heard of Fredfax. This is a *teletext* system in which a TV station transmits simultaneously with its normal programmes reproductions of pages of data such as the sports results, etc., which are held in the studio. The consumer's TV set, suitably modified, separates these simultaneous transmissions and displays either the normal programme or these pages — or both together if desired — as the viewer elects."

"But I'm only interested in the sports results," said Fred. "How can I just get them and cut out the rest of the rubbish?"

"Well, all the pages are transmitted sequentially but quickly.

All you have to do is select your page number by means of a control and when that page is received by your set it displays it to the exclusion of the others for as long as you wish."

"I've heard of something like this where you ring up, or something," said Fred vaguely.

"Ah, that's a different system. That's *viewdata*. True, they appear similar but there's a real difference — with viewdata you, the viewer, are connected by telephone direct to the studio and the data comes along your telephone lines to your set — not over the air as in teletext."

"Well what's the advantage of viewdata?" enquired Fred.

"The sheer volume of data accessible," replied Rufus. "Clearly, in the case of teletext there's a limit to the volume that can be transmitted over the air since the whole "book" of pages has to be transmitted over and over again. This means that teletext must restrict itself to the relatively more popular data. Viewdata, on the other hand, has no such access time limitation since the viewer's line is immediately hooked into the appropriate data address. This allows local and specialist information to be obtained as well as transitory information such as travel timetables and fare structures. Indeed, viewdata allows for private systems. In other words, a company could keep data in the studio which could be called up by the company's executives on TV screens anywhere in the country — or world, come to that."

"You mean a sales manager abroad could call up over the telephone for a TV display showing the stocks at the factory?"

"That's what we're coming to."

Data base — the Recording Angel on Earth

"That trick you mentioned earlier of having the product number alter a number of files on a real-time basis," said Fred. "I think that could be expanded, you know."

"My dear Fred, that 'trick', as you call it, is probably the most explosive concept in modern computer development. From it has evolved the whole technique of the *data base.*"

"Data base? I've heard of a data bank," said Fred uncertainly.

"A data bank is simply a large comprehensive store of data. But a data base is essentially a data bank which is so organised that the data *can be used for all sorts of applications* and is not limited to just one — such as seat reservations. The base is updated using a real-time technique and its data is available by terminal to all authorised personnel."

"Simple enough to imagine," sniffed Fred.

"It may be simple to imagine but it's very much harder to organise! You must appreciate, Fred, that a system whereby all related files are accessed at the same time so that a single input can immediately update all the files it affects requires several levels of control of a very high quality. To start with, it is crucial that the input data is rigorously edited — otherwise you'll have a situation that would make the cat-among-the-pigeons scenario look like a study of frozen immobility. Then the system design itself is hardly an exercise for beginners."

"I remember how complex our system design was for the kennels," mused Fred. "And then we were looking at essentially one procedure at a time."

"That's right. As a matter of fact you may also remember that we noted some over-lapping of procedures (such as TAKINGS and INVOICING routines) which suggested possible integration."

"But it was hard enough thinking of all the angles involved in a single procedure. I'd dread to think what would be involved if all the angles throughout the entire system had to be considered simultaneously."

"Well, that's the scale of a data base operation. Mind you, it teaches the hard lesson that the true object of data processing is *effective file management* as against mere computing."

"Which just goes to prove that any dunce can do mathematics but it takes a genius to keep a file," said Fred who rather fancied himself as a records clerk.

"And helps to explain why it takes longer to create a national data base than to put a man on the moon," added Rufus. "But it's coming, Fred, it's coming — of that you can be sure."

Down with Big Computer

"With all this increasing computerisation it looks as if I've a bright future," grinned Fred. But to his surprise Rufus replied with only a doubtful grunt.

"Depends on the growth of distributed processing, doesn't it?"

"Distributed processing? That anything like word processing?" asked Fred, an inexplicable forboding coming over him.

"No, it isn't. It's the term we used to describe a system in which the computer processing power is *physically* exactly where it's needed — on the shop-floor, in the storeroom and sales office, at the accountant's right hand, on the boardroom table. In other words, lots of little computers all over the place each doing its own thing — and very little central processing."

"Little central processing?" gasped an alarmed Fred. Visions of queues of redundant data processing managers floated before his eyes. "But, surely, the cost . . . and, after what you've just said about data bases . . . ."

"Costs?" Rufus dismissed these with a wave of his hand. "These days the cost of separate computers is less than the cost of the hassle with the DP department. But you do have a point about data bases. Ideally, integration between central and distributed processing is called for — you know, processing and validation of the data arising locally but supported by centralised data bases and high-power computing potential. Fancy yourself as an integrator, Fred?"

"Fancy myself more as a consumer," muttered Fred, and Rufus took the hint.

"Tell me," exclaimed Fred on his mentor's return. "This viewdata — would it by any chance have a page of Sits. Vac. . . . ?"

INDEX